BRANCH LINE TO UPWELL

Vic Mitchell Keith Smith
Andrew C Ingram

MP Middleton Press

This album is dedicated to Rev Wilbert Awdry and Rev Teddy Boston who worked so hard to keep the memory of the tramway alive.

First published November 1995

ISBN 1 873793 64 2

© *Middleton Press 1995*

Design - Deborah Goodridge

Published by Middleton Press
       Easebourne Lane
       Midhurst
       West Sussex
       GU29 9AZ
       Tel: 01730 813169
       Fax: 01730 812601

Printed & bound by Biddles Ltd,
       Guildford and Kings Lynn

CONTENTS

INDEX

ACKNOWLEDGEMENTS

In addition to information supplied by the photographers I am most grateful to the following for their assistance in the preparation of this book: D.Bailey, R.Bell, K.Bowden, R.Casserley, P.Crofts, S.Cousins, D.Cullen, W.Dawson, C.Garford, L.Heanes, L.Maywood, F.Means, D.Norman, C.Payne, M.Petty, T.Pleasance, N.Rand, S.Robb, M.Stallard, W.Taylor, J.Watling, the staff at Cambridge County Record Office, Cambridge University Library, Cambridgeshire Collection, National Railway Museum, Wisbech District Library, and Wisbech & Fenland Museum. A special word of thanks goes to the tramway staff for sharing their memories.

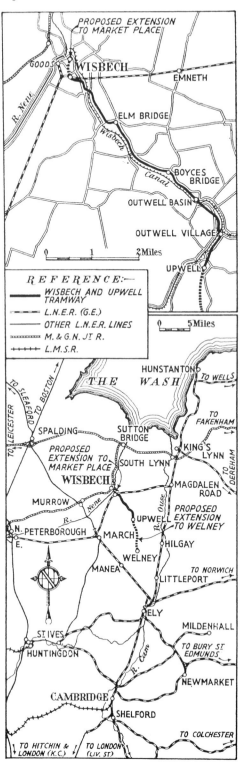

(Railway Magazine)

GEOGRAPHICAL SETTING

In the reign of William the Conqueror, when waterways were the chief means of transport, Wisbech was the gateway to The Fens. The earliest settlement was on the west bank of the river where a market for local produce had existed since Saxon times. Situated close to The Wash and flanked by the Well Stream and a small tributary of the Old Nene, the town was an obvious place for a Norman stronghold. By 1087 a stone castle stood on this fen island, which was later visited by King John who, according to Matthew Paris, a contemporary chronicler, lost his treasure whilst crossing the Well Stream.

The Well Stream originally carried the waters of the Ouse, Cam, Wissey and Old Nene from Upwell to the estuary at Wisbech. A new channel was cut from Littleport to Stowbridge around 1300, allowing the combined waters of the Cam, Ouse and Wissey to flow into The Wash at King's Lynn. The original northern branch of the Nene flowed from Peterborough to enter The Wash at Tydd Gote. A southern branch entered the Well Creek at Outwell to join the Ouse at Salter's Lode. In the 1470s Bishop Morton constructed a leam to take the waters of the original Nene from Peterborough through Guyhirn to Wisbech. With the flow of water between Outwell and Wisbech reduced, this section of the Well Stream silted up and gradually became extinct.

In the last 300 years drainage of The Fens and land reclamation from The Wash has resulted in Wisbech now standing 10 miles inland. River traffic on the present Nene increased dramatically following completion of the Nene Outfall Works between Wisbech and The Wash in 1831. The town's population also increased in the 19th century from 4,710 in 1801 to 9,808 by 1901.

All the maps are to the scale of 25ins to 1 mile, unless otherwise indicated.

HISTORICAL BACKGROUND

The aim of the Wisbech Canal Company's Act of 1794 was to reopen the Well Creek, thus restoring navigation between the Ouse and Nene. The work of dredging, straightening and widening over five miles of waterway was completed by the end of 1795.

A railway from Wisbech alongside the Wisbech Canal and Well Creek to Upwell had been proposed in 1873, but the scheme lacked sufficient funds. In 1880 the Great Eastern Railway decided to try an experiment: building the line as a standard gauge railway, but within the provisions of the 1870 Tramways Act. This allowed the line to be constructed with less stringent regulations, and therefore less expense, than a conventional railway. The experiment has resulted in a confused public still asking "was it a railway or a tramway".

The tramway opened on 20th August 1883, but services initially were only to Outwell. The extension to Upwell came into use on 8th September 1884.

Following the tramway opening, toll receipts on the canal fell steadily, with no dividend being paid to shareholders after 1896. Commercial traffic on the Wisbech Canal ceased in 1922, just five years before the tramway's passenger service was withdrawn on 31st December 1927, due to competition from road transport. The goods service continued however and eventually outlived the passenger service by 38 years. It enjoyed a period of great activity from 1945 to 1950 when petrol was rationed, with double-headed fruit trams of up to 60 vans becoming common in the season.

The tramway was completely closed on 23rd May 1966, with the line laying dormant until the track was finally lifted in Spring 1968. This album marks the bicentenary of the Canal's opening and the 30th anniversary of the Tramway's closure, the last roadside steam tramway in Britain.

PASSENGER SERVICES

Every Saturday "Whybrow's Boat" sailed from The Royal Inn at Wisbech, carrying passengers and cargo along the canal to Outwell and Upwell. The service had been withdrawn by 1892 as the newly-opened tramway offered a faster service for the same 2d fare.

In its early years of operation passengers on the Wisbech & Outwell Tramway were conveyed in carriages formerly used on the Millwall Extension Railway. A poster for October 1883 advertised six return journeys every weekday, a flat fare of 2d Third Class or 3d First Class, with the tram stopping to set down or pick up passengers at any point along the line. The early morning tram left Wisbech at 7.10am whilst the last one arrived back in town at 8.25pm.

Two four-wheeled tramcars were delivered to Wisbech in July 1884, with two bogie tramcars and a luggage van arriving in September for the commencement of through services to Upwell. The renamed Wisbech & Upwell Tramway ran six return trams, but with a revised 6.45am start and 10pm finish. A First Class ticket from Wisbech to Upwell cost 4d, but fares between Boyce's Bridge and Outwell Basin were slashed to 2d First Class and 1d Second Class. Four additional tramcars were supplied in June 1890 allowing the Millwall carriages to be withdrawn.

In 1902 the fares and level of service had remained unchanged since 1884, although the journey time for the six miles had been reduced from one hour to 50 minutes. Official figures for the years 1903 to 1914 show that an average of 120,572 passengers used the line each year, with a peak of 140,395 in 1905. By 1907 some fares had risen slightly and designated stopping places were introduced, the time-table now stating that "The tramcars will not stop at any other point along the line of route." The journey time had also been reduced to 39 minutes, and it stayed at this level for the remaining 20 years of passenger traffic. By 1922 a First Class ticket from Wisbech to Upwell cost 10d whilst the Boyce's Bridge to Outwell Basin fare had doubled to 2d, back to its 1883 price!

LOCOMOTIVES

The tramway's most distinctive feature has always been its motive power. The first three Worsdell 0-4-0T steam tram engines were built to Order Number G15 for the tramway's opening. Nos. 130 and 131 were completed at the Great Eastern Railway's Stratford Works in June 1883. One hauled a special on Monday 9th July 1883 when Major-General Hutchinson, the Board of Trade Inspector, visited the line. The third engine, no. 132, arrived in time for the tram's inaugural run on Saturday 20th August 1883. A further seven 0-4-0T tram engines were constructed between 1885 and 1897. Some were for use on the Yarmouth tramway although all ten locomotives spent part of their working lives at Wisbech.

In October 1903, a more powerful 0-6-0T version emerged from Stratford Works. Designed by James Holden and built to Order Number C53, this class closely resembled the G15 0-4-0Ts. The twelve locomotives were employed on shunting duties at Ipswich Docks, and on the quays at Yarmouth and Colchester, in addition to hauling goods on the tramway. In January 1922 only no. 131 was assigned to the tramway, but the allocation had risen to five by 1935.

In 1930, the LNER had over 50 Sentinel locomotives working successfully and ordered two special versions for the tramway. Each had a vertical water-tube boiler, two vertical engines and two-speed gearing. The drivers were unable to obtain success with them and they left after about six months use.

Following withdrawal in November 1952, no. 68083 was stored in Stratford Paint Shop with a view to preserving this last 0-4-0T tram engine. In December 1953 a report in the railway press stated that the locomotive "has disappeared and is believed to have been cut up". The question of its whereabouts was later raised on a BBC radio programme, with the local paper commenting "Could it be sheeted down in some remote siding? Has it become yet another ghost train?" In the 1980s stories circulated of a scrap merchant who had purchased a tram locomotive, burnt off the wooden superstructure, but never got around to cutting it up. According to the story it still languishes in a shed near Ipswich!

The prototype Drewry diesel shunter no. DS1173 ran trials on the tramway and other LNER lines before finding a permanent home on the Southern Region in 1948. Four production locomotives nos. 11100-3 were built for Drewry in 1952 by the Vulcan Foundry Co Ltd. Following standard practice for all Wisbech & Upwell locomotives the diesels were fitted with front and rear cowcatchers, side valancing and a speed governor.

1. Canal: Sluice Bridge towards Elm Road
SLUICE BRIDGE

2. A rare view from the River Nene of Sluice Bridge crossing the entrance to Wisbech Canal. In addition to providing its water supply, the Nene also deposited silt, which created problems for the canal throughout its existence. Each retreating tide left more mud requiring a progressively higher tide to fill the waterway. (Wisbech & Fenland Museum)

←

1. A Wisbech Castle has stood within The Crescent for over nine hundred years. Each of the four buildings has replaced its predecessor on the same site, which was strategically positioned near the confluence of the River Nene and former Well Stream. This wartime photograph was taken from 2500ft by the RAF on Monday 28th July 1941.
(Wisbech & Fenland Museum)

The 1903 edition of the 6in to 1 mile map shows the Wisbech Canal from top to bottom,

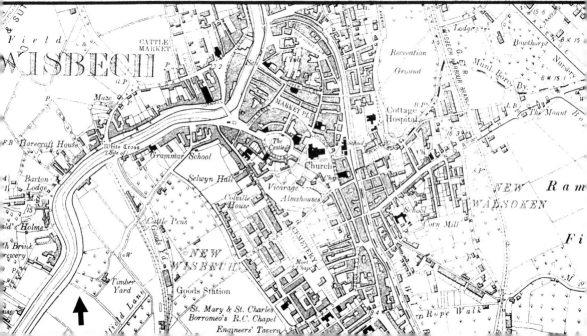

3. The mud by Wisbech Sluice was described in 1807 as the greatest evil facing the canal company. In this 1929 view a fishing smack is moored in The Neck, a short length of tidal waterway between Sluice Bridge and Wisbech Sluice. In the distance can be glimpsed the lantern of the Octagon Church, demolished in 1952. (Cambridgeshire Collection, Cambridgeshire Libraries)

5. In winter, fen folk would skate to market along the canal, taking care to avoid thin ice under bridges, and frozen reeds. Snow cleared from Wisbech streets was tipped into the canal, so with wellingtons, skates, walking sticks and oil drums these local youngsters enjoy a game of ice hockey. On one occasion the sluice keeper was mobbed by an angry crowd after he had let water into the canal, spoiling the ice.
(Lilian Ream Exhibition Gallery)

4. After the canal had been abandoned as a through waterway, a concrete culvert was constructed under Sluice Bridge with a penstock gate at each end. Following completion in September 1930, the County Council announced that it should now be possible to flush out the canal with fresh water, thus eliminating some of the nuisance that had existed owing to stagnation. (Lilian Ream Exhibition Gallery)

WISBECH SLUICE

6. Built of oak with elm planking a Fenland Lighter was about 42ft long with a 10ft-11ft beam at deck level. Following Benson Woodward's death in 1880 Robert Pogson was appointed Sluice Keeper. His whitewashed cottage stands beside Wisbech Sluice, which was equipped with two pair of navigation gates and two pair of sea gates. This is the only known photograph of a vessel on the Wisbech Canal. (Wisbech & Fenland Museum)

7. At a Marshland Rural District Council meeting in 1933, Councillor Bettinson stated that "if they had the canal filled up they would have a wonderful roadway." This nightmare came true for here is Churchill Road at the same location as picture no. 6. Note the house, now demolished, on the extreme right of both photographs. (Wisbech & Fenland Museum)

BLACKFRIAR'S BRIDGE

8. There were originally eight road bridges across the canal between Wisbech and Outwell, of which seven followed this same basic design. Blackfriar's Bridge, seen here circa 1897, linked Blackfriar's Road and Ruby Street. The two buildings on the left were the only structures in this photograph still standing by 1995. (Lilian Ream Exhibition Gallery)

Wisbech Sluice Toll Receipts

	£	s	d		£	s	d
1796	212	17	0	1865	232	14	10
1800	408	16	11	1870	229	5	5
1805	689	6	2	1875	150	8	1
1810	359	16	4	1880	128	1	7
1815	674	9	5	1885	106	4	5
1820	358	12	0	1890	96	1	3
1825	249	6	10	1895	101	16	9
1830	149	13	0	1900	42	14	8
1835	165	6	0	1905	11	8	4
1840	189	1	0	1910	46	7	2
1845	349	12	4	1915	23	16	6
1850	406	11	9	1920	0	0	0
1855	474	18	6	1922	0	0	0
1860	323	12	7				

9. The canal had been open for over 100 years before Blackfriar's Bridge was rebuilt. Wisbech Corporation adopted a lattice girder design, which at 22ft 6in wide was about double the width of the old bridge. Rebuilt in six weeks using white bricks with blue brick coping, it opened for traffic without ceremony on Thursday 15th August 1901. (Cambridgeshire Collection, Cambridgeshire Libraries)

10. The 1849 cholera epidemic in Wisbech, which resulted in 47 deaths, was attributed to drinking water obtained from the river and canal. Residents of Wellington Terrace survey the abandoned waterway in 1927, whilst trying to ignore the stench from decaying vegetation. In the mid-1950s, a local businessman offered to restore the canal between Wisbech Sluice and New Common Bridge as a leisure waterway, but this was rejected by the council. (Lilian Ream Exhibition Gallery)

WALSOKEN BRIDGE

The Bench Mark on this 1889 edition shows that Walsoken Bridge, at 24.43ft above sea level, was one of the highest points in Wisbech.

11. On the right bank behind Walsoken Bridge stands The Ferry Boat Inn, where a ferry once plied across the broad estuary of the Well Stream. In 1948 a local photographer moved into the tall building on the left. His business was relocated in 1967 as the site was required for road improvements. As demolition work progressed the rubble, and all his negatives, crashed into the canal.
(Wisbech & Fenland Museum)

Order of Service for the reopening and
renaming of Walsoken Bridge on Saturday
9th August 1902.

Walsoken Bridge

Meet at Town Hall at   9.45
Leave there   10.15
reach Walsoken Bridge 10.40

A short Prayer will be offered by the Vicar.

The Mayor will then address Miss Susanna Peckover.

The Rev^d J Young as Chairman of the Walsoken District
Council will also address Miss Susanna Peckover.
The Mayor and Miss Peckover walk over the Bridge.
The Mayor will formally ask Miss Peckover to declare the
Bridge open.
Miss Peckover will please say, I declare this Bridge open.

The Mayor will ask Miss Peckover if she wishes the Bridge
to be known by any particular name.
       Miss Peckover will please reply
                    Coronation Bridge
                    Coronation Bridge Road
The Mayor repeats those names and states that it is in
commemoration of the Coronation of King Edward the Seventh.

The Mayor asks for three cheers for the King

and also three cheers the the kind donor of the Bridge.

12. Miss Susanna Peckover, a member of the local banking family, donated £1200 towards the rebuilding of Walsoken Bridge. At a service in 1902 led by the Rector of Walsoken, Rev John Young (centre), she unveiled a tablet to commemorate the coronation of King Edward VII. The Coronation - and therefore the opening of the bridge - had to be postponed from 26th June until 9th August because of the King's operation for acute appendicitis. (Wisbech & Fenland Museum)

13. In 1940, Royal Engineers posted beside each of the bridges had orders to destroy them with high explosives if Hitler invaded England and attempted to cross Wisbech Canal. Every time the air-raid siren sounded, a sapper had to run to the Police Station for a plunger and detonator, which were then returned following the all-clear. (C.Aldrich coll.)

14. This is the view south from Coronation Bridge along Napier Terrace in the late 1940s. The canal waters claimed many lives through tragic accidents and suicides. This also may be the very spot, according to Gardiner's *History of Wisbech*, where King John lost his treasure on 12th October 1216 whilst crossing the Well Stream. Unfortunately for treasure-seekers this is now a dual carriageway. (R.Fairhead)

WISBECH CANAL.

THIS is to Certify, that *Edward Goodger of Wisbech Saint Peters in the Isle of Ely Basket Maker* is intitled to one Share, No. **30** of the Navigation called the *WISBECH CANAL*, and of all Benefit and Advantage to arise therefrom.   Given under the Common Seal of the Company at their Second General Assembly holden at *Wisbech* on the 8th Day of May, 1795.

THE · SEAL
WISBECH
COMPANY
ANNO
OF · THE
CANAL
INCORPOR ED
1794

15. A tow path ran the length of the canal as haulage was principally by horses, although in later years steam power was occasionally used. The former steam-powered corn mill in Elm Road is dwarfed by the mature beech and chestnut trees. In 1943, the Wisbech Advertiser reported that a crocodile had been seen in the canal. It transpired that some boys had earlier broken into Wisbech Museum, and that the reptile floating down the waterway was stuffed! (Cambridgeshire Collection, Cambridgeshire Libraries)

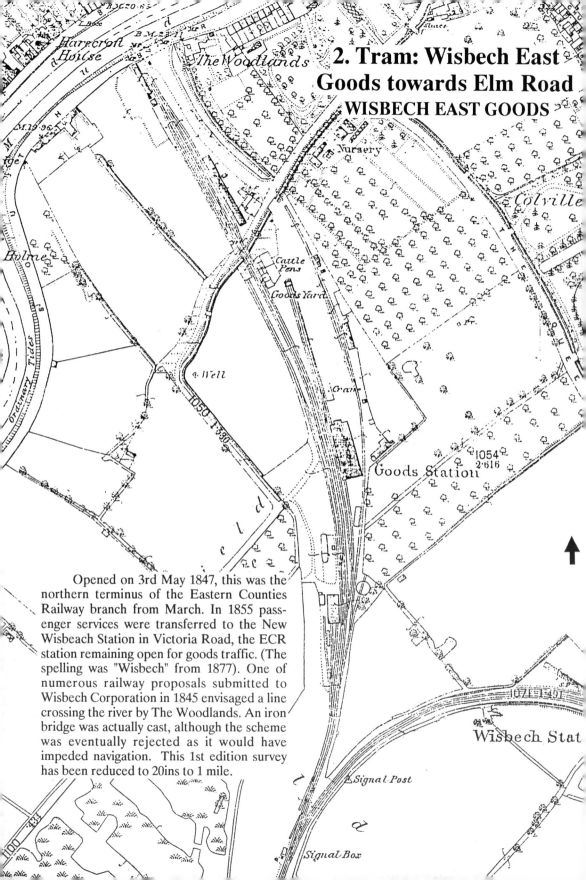

2. Tram: Wisbech East Goods towards Elm Road
WISBECH EAST GOODS

Opened on 3rd May 1847, this was the northern terminus of the Eastern Counties Railway branch from March. In 1855 passenger services were transferred to the New Wisbech Station in Victoria Road, the ECR station remaining open for goods traffic. (The spelling was "Wisbech" from 1877). One of numerous railway proposals submitted to Wisbech Corporation in 1845 envisaged a line crossing the river by The Woodlands. An iron bridge was actually cast, although the scheme was eventually rejected as it would have impeded navigation. This 1st edition survey has been reduced to 20ins to 1 mile.

16. Wisbech East Goods was by far the busiest GER station in the area. Between June and October 1922 15609 tons of fruit were dispatched by goods and passenger train, a significant proportion coming from the tramway. This photograph was taken from the Somers Road entrance with the Weighbridge Office on the right. (J.Mews coll.)

17. Chip baskets of fruit from Mr Baker of Emneth are stacked on the floor of GE Fruit Van no. 1836, bound for Bradford market. The art of loading large numbers of strawberry chips was to stack them in a pyramid which prevented the chips sliding during shunting. (J.Mews coll.)

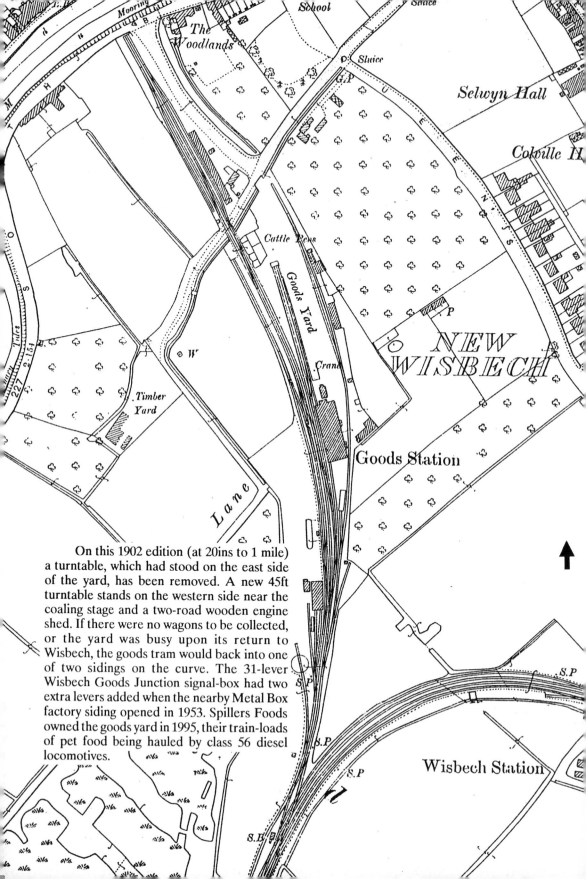

Mooring

School

Sluice

The Woodlands

Sluice

Selwyn Hall

Colville H.

Cattle Pens

Goods Yard

NEW
WISBECH

Crane

W

Timber
Yard

Goods Station

Lane

On this 1902 edition (at 20ins to 1 mile) a turntable, which had stood on the east side of the yard, has been removed. A new 45ft turntable stands on the western side near the coaling stage and a two-road wooden engine shed. If there were no wagons to be collected, or the yard was busy upon its return to Wisbech, the goods tram would back into one of two sidings on the curve. The 31-lever Wisbech Goods Junction signal-box had two extra levers added when the nearby Metal Box factory siding opened in 1953. Spillers Foods owned the goods yard in 1995, their train-loads of pet food being hauled by class 56 diesel locomotives.

S.P

S.P

S.P

S.B

S.P

Wisbech Station

S.B

18. The single main-line passenger engine allocated to this depot stands beside the coaling stage with the station pilot, J70 no. 7137. The Wisbech East pilot, usually a tram engine or J15 0-6-0, would work the Wisbech East Harbour branch, occasionally together. Tram engines also hauled a water truck between Coldham and Middle Drove to supply crossing cottages. (Lens of Sutton)

19. A simple magneto party line connected Wisbech East Goods and the tram depots. With one ring to call Wisbech, two for Elm Bridge, three for Boyce's Bridge etc, staff could telephone any location to pass on instructions. The site of Wisbech's first railway station is now its last link with the national network but the station offices, seen here in September 1981, have now been demolished. (A.C.Ingram)

20. The telegraph pole was there first, then in 1961 Coote & Warren requested a siding to serve their new coal wharf. Their plan was obviously followed to the letter. When departing for Upwell the tram engine would propel its wagons from the yard onto the up main line at Wisbech Goods Junction. It then ran wrong road towards Wisbech East Passenger. Alternatively the pilot engine would haul the train onto the up main with the tram engine coupling up at the far end. (Lilian Ream Exhibition Gallery)

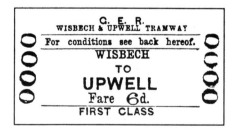

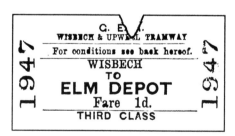

Tickets issued by the Booking Office at Wisbech Station. Passengers boarding the tram at other locations purchased tram-style tickets from the conductor-guard.

VICTORIA ROAD CROSSING

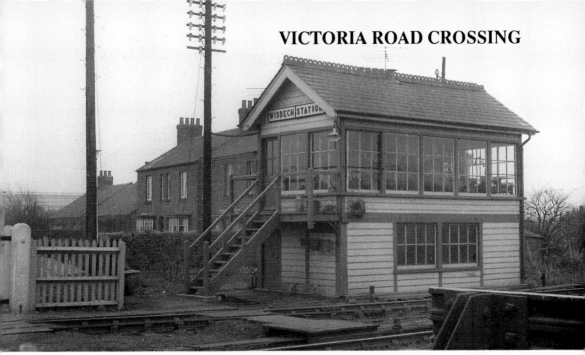

21. Wisbech Station signal-box controlled main line and tramway movements within the station area - there were no signals on the actual tramway. The signalman would stand on the trackside wooden platform to collect a tablet pouch from trains leaving the single-track up main line.
(J.Stafford-Baker/A.C.Ingram)

22. The Tyer's Apparatus by the window issued tablets for the single-line section between Wisbech and Emneth. The 32-lever frame, shunting signals and point rodding were removed by volunteers from the North Norfolk Railway on Sunday 1st June 1969.
(A.C.Ingram)

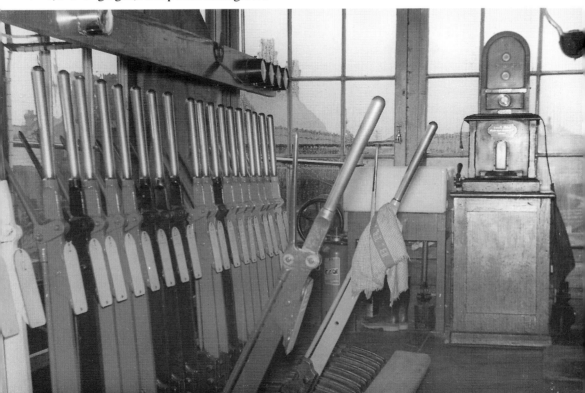

23. The steps have already gone, and now the walkway of GER bridge no. 2320 is lifted off its piers by a steam breakdown crane on Sunday 19th February 1961. This bridge had provided pedestrian access between Victoria Road and Railway Road when the level crossing gates were closed. (Lilian Ream Exhibition Gallery)

24. Dr Ian Allen once travelled on the footplate to Wisbech with Driver Charlie Rand, then realised his car was still parked at Outwell! On a later visit he photographed D2201 entering Wisbech East on the high-level tramway road, alongside the overgrown sidings at Wisbech Tram Shed. (I.C.Allen/C.Moss)

WISBECH TRAM SHED

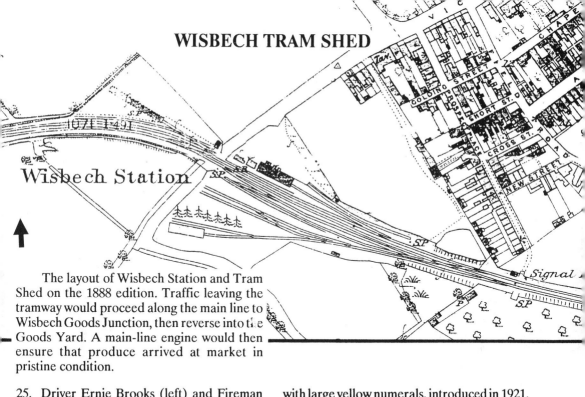

The layout of Wisbech Station and Tram Shed on the 1888 edition. Traffic leaving the tramway would proceed along the main line to Wisbech Goods Junction, then reverse into the Goods Yard. A main-line engine would then ensure that produce arrived at market in pristine condition.

25. Driver Ernie Brooks (left) and Fireman Steve Culley are on the footplate with Jack Ogden standing beside no. 132, one of three class G15 0-4-0Ts delivered to Wisbech for the tramway's opening in August 1883. The livery is crimson lake woodwork, grey metalwork with large yellow numerals, introduced in 1921. This was the only member of the trio taken into LNER stock as Class Y6. Renumbered 7132 in 1924 she was withdrawn on 21st October 1931. (National Railway Museum)

Statement shewing Locomotive and Carriage Expenses in connection with
Wisbech and Upwell Tramway, Year ended December 31st 1914.

General Repairs and Maintenance of Engines and Cars	£	s	d
Engines	258	12	0
Cars	164	12	0
	£423	4	2

Cost of Traction Power	£	s	d
Fuel	392	12	4
Drivers and Firemen	674	14	5
Lubricants	23	17	10
Cleaners, Coalmen, etc	73	2	5
Other Stores	17	14	6
Water	53	1	6
	£1235	3	0

Depreciation	£	s	d
Engines	165	5	4
Tram Cars	99	3	2
	£264	8	6

Total Expenditure plus depreciation	£1922	15	8

	Passenger	Goods & Coal		Total
Train Miles	23136	16522		39664
	Engines	Cars		
Working Stock	6	10		

Milage of Cars

No.1	No.2	No.3	No.4	No.5	No.6	No.7	No.8	No.16 Brake	Ordy Bk.Vans	Total
4620	4168	3420	6576	9672	14560	10444	8020	19976	3180	84636

26. Entering service on the Yarmouth tramway in October 1885, this locomotive differed from no. 132 by having sliding side windows inside the body, and window frames with rounded top corners. It was working on the Wisbech & Upwell Tramway by 1900 but in January 1921 no. 129 was placed on the GER duplicate list as no. 0129. The original number was reused on a new 0-6-0T tram engine then under construction.
(National Railway Museum)

27. Adapted for the tramway, LNER class Y10 Sentinels had a vertical boiler (left), two enclosed engines (right) and chain drive. One driver recalled they were poor steamers whilst another remembered that "they smoked like a battleship." No. 8404 arrived on 11th September 1930 and left for Yarmouth on 8th May 1931. This view at Wisbech Tram Shed in January 1931 is the first authenticated photograph of a Y10 on the tramway. (W.Whitworth/A.Garraway coll.)

28. Driver Jack Ogden is coaling up his tram engine at Wisbech in 1937. Staff could earn extra money by unloading coal from wagons onto the stage for a shilling a ton. A 138ft long wooden tramcar shed had previously stood beside the depot. Locomotives were later stored on this site and pressed into service during the busy fruit season. (H.G.Ellis)

29. J70 no. 7136 is receiving attention inside the shed in June 1937. Charlie Rand began his career on the tramway cleaning engines in the shed by the light of oil lamps. At 4am he would knock up the driver and mate for duty at 5am. He recalled "when the driver came on duty he would look at the engine, then he would wipe different parts with a cloth. If it was dirty you would clean it again." (R.F.Roberts)

30. Here is a rare interior view of the same locomotive looking along the boiler towards the firebox end in 1939. The J70s were fitted with a 180psi Diagram 46 boiler driving 3ft 1in wheels through two outside cylinders. They were also reputed to be the first British standard gauge locomotives to be fitted with Walschaerts valve gear. (P.Erwood)

31. J70 nos. 7128, 8217 and Y6 no. 8083 stand quietly on the old tramcar road whilst J70 no. 8218 and Y6 no. 8082 brew up outside the shed on 2nd July 1946. The GER slotted signal was for the high-level tram road from Wisbech Station to the Goods Junction. (A.F.Cook)

32. Class J70 no. 8225 was transferred from Ipswich Docks to the tramway on 5th June 1949. Renumbered 68225 in May 1950 it stayed on the tramway until the end of steam, apart from a three-month spell in 1951 shunting the Hythe Quay at Colchester. The King's Lynn-based 0-6-0T stabled at the shed would be employed as a pilot in the East Goods Yard. (National Railway Museum)

Statement of the Earnings of the WISBECH & UPWELL TRAMWAY
Year Ended 31st December 1914

	£	s	d
Passengers	1337	7	10
Mails	16	0	0
Parcels up to 2cwt, &c	37	10	6
Other merchandise by Pass'r Train	55	8	3
Merchandise	3923	4	4
Live Stock	51	8	0
Coal &c	343	4	6
Other Minerals	329	18	10
Rents	31	12	1
Total £6125		14	4

Number of Passengers
1st Class   3,547
3rd Class 114,340
        Total 117,887
Note:- Return tickets counted as two

33. The 23ft high water tower was at the entrance to Wisbech Tram Shed yard. The signal on the left controlled departure from the high-level tram platform, whilst the GER shunting signal by the water column guarded access to the tramway from the low-level avoiding line. (J.Stafford-Baker/A.C.Ingram)

Copy of official plans dated 26th August 1895. Scale: 3mm to 1ft. (Wisbech & Fenland Museum)

34. Class J70 no. 68222 is taking water prior to working the 12.45pm goods tram to Upwell on Wednesday 7th June 1950. With only about half the water capacity of a J69 0-6-0T the tram engines would have their tanks topped up before every journey. This locomotive carries the British Railways livery of brown woodwork and black metalwork with white or cream lettering. (M.N.Bland)

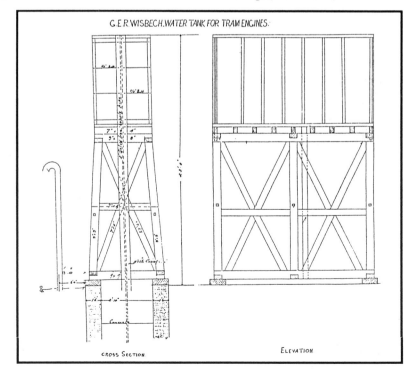

G.E.R.WISBECH.WATER TANK FOR TRAM ENGINES.

CROSS SECTION

ELEVATION

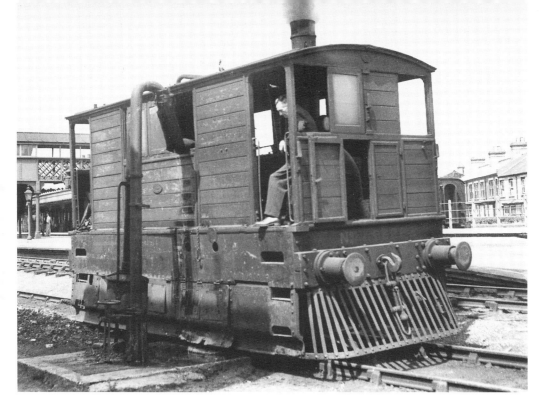

35.   Fireman Arthur Banyard (right) is with Driver Albert South who joined the tramway staff in 1918 as a cleaner. Working through the grades, Albert fired the last passenger tram in December 1927 and drove the last goods tram in May 1966. No. 68222 was transferred to Colchester on 21st June 1953 and Ipswich five months later on 15th November. It was finally withdrawn from service on 31st January 1955. (National Railway Museum)

36.   This was the first of four diesel loco-motives that worked on the tramway at various times between 1952 and 1966. No. 11102 leaves the shed yard to haul the 12.55pm tram to Upwell on 4th June 1952. It was later fitted with a thin exhaust stack and renumbered D2202 in January 1958. Sister locomotive D2203 is now preserved on the Yorkshire Dales Railway at Embsay. (M.N.Bland)

37.   Wisbech Tram Shed yard was photo-graphed in the early 1960s from the tramway platform, which was just 1ft 2in above rail level. Diesels were stabled in the old steam shed for some years until the right-hand side was demolished and the left-hand bay reroofed. (J.Stafford-Baker/A.C.Ingram)

WISBECH EAST PASSENGER

38. This is the only known photograph of New Wisbeach Station, opened by the Eastern Counties Railway in 1855. It replaced a temporary wooden structure opened by the East Anglian Railway on 1st February 1848. Horse-drawn carriages from the Rose & Crown, White Hart and White Lion hotels would meet every train. The sign *This way to the Tramcars* dates this view between 1883 and 1888. (Wisbech & Fenland Museum)

Brass-rubbing from 8in x 5in worksplate off first production Drewry shunter no. 11100. Allocated to March depot between September 1962 and August 1964 this locomotive was noted working the Harbour Branch, and no doubt also took turns of duty on the tramway.

Considering that a First Class ticket on the Wisbech & Outwell Tramway cost 3d, the fare for one bicycle seems exorbitant. (M.Elston coll.)

39. Plans by the GER in its General Powers Act of 24th July 1882 to extend the tramway into Wisbech Market Place were later dropped, much to the dismay of the Town Council. In May 1888 the Great Eastern Railway commenced work on a new station building. The old station was demolished on 27th August with Phase One of the new structure opening on Monday 3rd December. The remaining wooden up platform was then replaced by a new island platform that opened in Spring 1889. (National Railway Museum)

This 1902 edition shows the remodelled Wisbech station and tram shed. A new signal-box stands on the far side of Victoria Road Crossing, now spanned by the footbridge. The tramcar shed has moved from Plot 246 to stand beside the engine shed, which was enlarged to two roads in 1893.

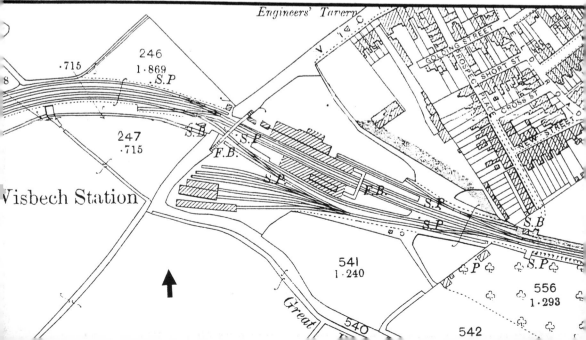

Estimate of New Station & Station Buildings at Wisbech	£	s	d
General and preliminary items	47	11	6
Excavator, bricklayer and drainage	1554	16	7
Mason, slate Mason, etc	321	13	7
Slater	87	14	11
Carpenter	391	6	5
Joiner & Ironmonger	422	17	1
Founder, Smith, etc	501	8	1
Plumber	521	0	8
Plasterer	165	12	11
Glazier	87	12	3
Painter	204	18	3
	4306	12	3
Surveyors Charges	61	10	0
	4368	2	3

Drower & Rusult, 17 Southampton Street, Bloomsbury Square, WC

The original document has a mathematical error in
the final total, which it gives as £4367 12s 3d.

40. Townsfolk gather at the western end of Wisbech Station in August 1914 to bid farewell to the first troop train of WWI, hauled by class E4 2-4-0 no. 438. Signalman Arthur Barrett stands by the level crossing looking up towards his signal-box. The larger brick building on the down platform is the former signal-box reduced to a single storey. (L.Baxter coll.)

41. After World War I, Charlie Robb bought a number of old Tilling buses from the London General Omnibus Co, and in 1920 commenced his Outwell Bus Service in direct competition with the tramway. His fleet stands near the proposed tramway terminus with a Robin Tea Charity excursion to Hunstanton. As they approached their destination half the passengers would get out and walk as the buses could not carry a full load up Heacham Hill. (J.Robb coll.)

Framed notice placed above the doorway
inside each tramcar. (M.Gates coll.)

L. N. E. R.

PASSENGERS ARE NOT ALLOWED TO TRAVEL ON THE OUTSIDE PLATFORM OF THE CAR, AND ARE CAUTIONED NOT TO ATTEMPT TO ALIGHT FROM THE CAR WHILE IN MOTION.

42. LNER class Y6 0-4-0T no. 7133 beside footbridge no. 2321 in the mid-1920s with a mixed tram for Upwell. The leading vehicle is a Great Northern horsebox whilst the other is of North Eastern Railway origin. The locomotive's livery is brown woodwork and black metalwork with red bufferbeams and buffers. In July 1925 this locomotive took part in the Stockton & Darlington Railway Centenary procession as Exhibit no. 35. (National Railway Museum)

43. Class Y1 no. 8401 takes a brief trial on the Tramway. Seen here with a 4-wheeled tramcar, the Sentinel had been fitted with a Westing-house brake for working the passenger trams. The pair stand opposite the tram platform on Wednesday 4th May 1927. (R.H.R.Garraway)

44. Families from London's East End arrive at Wisbech for the 1933 fruit-picking season. The pickers would sleep in a bunkhouse and during the day female Cambridge undergraduates from Girton and Newnham Colleges would run creches for the under-10s. Students slept in tented camps scattered among the fruit farms and in the evenings attempted to brighten the hard lives of the pickers by organising services and socials.
(Lilian Ream Exhibition Gallery)

L.N.E.R.

M 9801

LUGGAGE.

From

To WISBECH

45. Driver Jack Ogden, Fireman Jim Dowling and Guard Fred Cole with J70 no. 8223 use the avoiding line through Wisbech East station on Tuesday 24th August 1948. Built in June 1914 as GER Class C53 no. 131, this locomotive was renumbered twice by the LNER, as no. 7131 in 1924 and no. 8223 in September 1946. (E.Woods)

46. The 9in x 5in brass worksplate from class J70 no. 8223 still carries the number 7131, although some other trams had their plates recast. (A.C.Ingram)

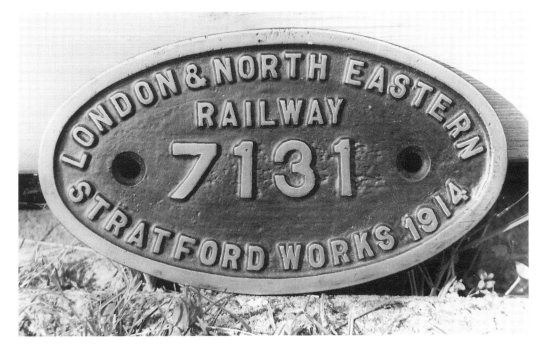

47. At 12.45pm on Friday 25th August 1950 an apparently driverless J70 no. 68217 passes through Wisbech East on the up main line, bound for Upwell. The down tram arrived in Upwell at 2pm after clearing Outwell Village of outgoing goods. These vans would then join the up tram which cleared the goods traffic from Outwell Basin, Boyce's Bridge and Elm Bridge. (H.C.Casserley)

TIME TABLE OF TRAMCARS & GOODS TRIPS BETWEEN WISBECH & UPWELL.

Single Line. For regulations and bye laws for working this tramway see "Appendix" to the Working Time Tables.

DOWN WEEK DAYS.

Miles M.C.		DAILY					MONDAYS TO FRIDAYS													SATURDAYS									
		1	2	3	4	5	6	7	8	9	10	11	12	13	14	15	16	17	18	19	20	21	22	23	24	25	26	27	28
		Gds.	Pass.	Pass.			Pass.	Gds.	Pass.	Gds.	Pass.	Gds.	Pass.	Pass. WR	Pass.	Pass.	Pass.			Gds.	Gds.	Pass.	Pass.	Pass.	Pass.	Pass.			
		a.m.	a.m.	a.m.			a.m.	a.m.	p.m.	p.m.	p.m.	p.m.	p.m.	p.m.	p.m.	p.m.	p.m.			a.m.	a.m.	a.m.	p.m.	p.m.	p.m.	p.m.			
— —	Wisbech Station ..... ⑤ dep.	6 30	7 55	9 30			10 55	11 5	12 40	12 45	2 13	2 25	2 45	5 32	6 45	8 0	8 30			10 55	11 30	11 55	3 5	5 32	7 20	9 0			
1 53	Elm Depot .... „	6 50	8 6	9 41			11 6	11 40	12 51	1 15	2 25	2 39	2 56	5 43	6 56	8 11	8 41			11 20	11 50	12 6	3 16	5 43	7 31	9 11			
3 25	Boyce's Depot .... ⑤ {arr.	7 0	8 15	9 50			11 15	11 50	1 0	1 23		3 5	5 52	7 5	8 20	8 50			11 30	12 0	12 15	3 25	5 52	7 40	9 20				
	{dep.	7 5	8 19	9 51			11 16	11 55	1 1	1 50	2 34	2 48	3 6	5 53	7 6	8 21	8 51			11 35	12 19	12 16	3 26	5 53	7 41	9 21			
4 12	Outwell Basin .... „	7 20	8 22	9 57			11 22	12 10	1 7	1 59	2 40	2 54	3 12	5 59	7 12	8 27	8 57			11 50	12 35	12 22	3 32	5 59	7 47	9 27			
4 79	Outwell Village .... „	7 54	8 28	10 3			11 28	12 24	1 13	2	2 69	3 10	3 18	6 5	7 18	8 33	9 3			11 56	12 51	12 28	3 38	6 5	7 53	9 33			
5 72	Upwell .... ⑤ arr.	8 0	8 34	10 9			11 34	12 30	1 19	2 16	3 6	3 16	3 24	6 11	7 24	8 39	9			12 26	1 0	12 34	3 44	6 11	7 59	9 39			

→14 & 16 Will not run after 31st August. →13 & 15 Commences 1st September. 20 To shunt at Boyce's Depot for 21.

UP WEEK DAYS.

Miles M.C.		DAILY					MONDAYS TO FRIDAYS												SATURDAYS									
		1	2	3	4	5	6	7	8	9	10	11	12	13	14	15	16	17	18	19	20	21	22	23	24	25	26	27	28
		Pass.	Gds.	Pass.			Pass.	Pass.	Pass. WR	Gds.	Pass.	Gds.	Gds.	Pass.	Pass.	Pass.	Pass.			Pass.	Gds.	Gds.	Pass.	Pass.	Pass.	Pass.			
		a.m.	a.m.	a.m.			a.m.	p.m.	p.m.	p.m.	p.m.	p.m.	p.m.	p.m.	p.m.	p.m.	p.m.			p.m.	p.m.	p.m.	p.m.	p.m.	p.m.	p.m.			
— —	Upwell .... ⑤ dep.	8 35	9 15	10 15			11 40	1 25	1 28	3 32	3 05	3 60	4 15	6 19	7 32	8 50	9 20			1 3	1 25	1 50	4 0	6 16	8 11	9 45			
73	Outwell Village .... „	8 41	9 30	10 21			11 46	1 31	1 35	3 38	3 41	4 25	4 40	6 22	7 38	8 56	9 26			1 9	1 31	2 15	4 12	6 22	8 17	9 51			
1 60	Outwell Basin .... „	8 47	9 40	10 27			11 52	1 37	1 44	3 44	4 5	4 45	5 0	6 28	7 44	9 2	9 32			1 15	1 50	2 25	4 18	6 28	8 17	9 57			
2 47	Boyce's Depot .... ⑤ {arr.	8 52	9 45	10 32			11 57	1 42	1 49	3 49	4 11	4 50	5 5	6 33	7 49	9 7	9 37			1 20	2	2 35	4 23	6 33	8 22	10 2			
	{dep.	8 53	9 52	10 33			11 58	1 43	1 50	3 50	4 16	4 51	5 6	6 34	7 50	9 8	9 38			1 21	2 6	2 36	4 24	6 34	8 23	10 3			
4 19	Elm Depot .... „		9 3	10 18	10 43			12 8	1 53	2 0	4 0	5 5	5 9	5 19	6 44	8 0	9 18	9 48			1 31	2 31	5 49	4 34	6 44	8 33	10 13			
5 72	Wisbech Station ..... ⑤ arr.	9 14	10 33	10 54			12 19	2 4	2 11	4 11	5 15	5 20	5 30	6 55	8 11	8 29	9 59			1 42	2 42	3 0	4 45	6 55	8 44	10 24			

→14 & 16 Will not run after 31st August. →13 & 15 Commences 1st September.

In addition to the above stopping places, the tram cars will also stop at the following points if required, for the purpose of taking up or setting down passengers, viz.:—Elm Road Crossing, New Common Bridge (Canal Bridge), Rose Cottage, Duke of Wellington Junction, Inglethorpe Hall, Collett's Bridge, Shepherd's Cottage, Dial House, Basin Gate, Horn's Corner, Goodman's Crossing, and Small Lode. The tram cars will not stop at any other point along the line of route.

No coal trucks are to be worked by any of the above tram-car trains. A special trip is to be run for the working of such traffic.

When required, SPECIAL TRIPS for conveying the coal traffic will be run between Wisbech and Upwell during the night. The Wisbech Station Master to arrange and advise all concerned.

The loads of the Wisbech and Upwell Passenger trams must not exceed 9 vehicles.

Loads of Goods and Coal trains.—The loads of goods and coal trains over the Wisbech and Upwell Tramway may be increased as under:—
For ordinary purposes four-coupled tram engine loads:—
10 mineral ; 15 goods ; 22 empties.
and for six-coupled tram engines for ordinary purposes the loads should be:—
15 mineral ; 22 goods ; 33 empties.
These loads may, however, be increased to meet special exigencies. The D.S.O. to arrange.

Tram Cars Nos. 7 and 8 each to be counted as 2 vehicles.
N.B.—Not exceeding 2 Through trucks from Wisbech to Upwell, and from Upwell to Wisbech may be worked in rear of a passenger tram.

The engine, after dusk, is to carry one red light and one white light in front, and the last vehicle is to carry one red light in rear.

48. The gardens and tram platform are seen from the Railway Road side of the footbridge on 4th June 1952. Rev Teddy Boston, who moved to Wisbech in 1950, was a ardent railway enthusiast and often travelled on the footplate wearing his cassock and dog collar. Charlie Rand recalled the occasion when Teddy shunted wagons into the middle siding beside Wisbech Shed. "He gave them such a wallop that they demolished the buffer-stops". The official explanation given to Station Master Rose was that the engine had slipped. It would not have been in Charlie's best interests to reveal that the Curate of St Peter's Church had been driving! (B.I.Nathan)

49. The eastern approach to Wisbech from the Harbour Goods brake van on 8th March 1951. Wisbech East station closed following withdrawal of the March to King's Lynn passenger service on 9th September 1968. Demolition work commenced on Wednesday 5th May 1971 with two gallons of diesel and a match. Paperwork dating back to the 1855 station and some tramway relics were rescued before the building went up in flames. (M.N.Bland)

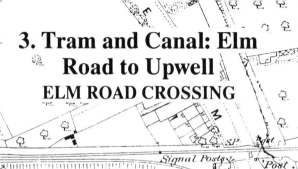

3. Tram and Canal: Elm Road to Upwell
ELM ROAD CROSSING

The King's Lynn line and tramway diverged at this point, some 440 yards east of Wisbech station. This 1888 map shows the original position of Wisbech Harbour Junction signal-box on the east side of Wisbech Canal.

50. In the distance cars pass the main-line gates, but the tram emerged from a separate gate by the signalman's cottage. In winter frozen mud between the running and check rails created problems for locomotives, whilst many cyclists recall being thrown off their machines at this ungated crossing. (J.Stafford-Baker/A.C.Ingram)

51. Situated between Elm Road and the canal, Wisbech Harbour Junction signal-box was responsible for the harbour branch and Elm Road crossings. Trams to Upwell were protected either by Elm Road main-line gates or a flagman. When the signalman saw a tram approaching from Upwell he would inform Wisbech Station box, as there was no telephone communication between the depots and signal-boxes. (J.Stafford-Baker/A.C.Ingram)

52. The Wisbech to King's Lynn line crossed the canal on GER bridge no. 2322. In 1927 the Wisbech Advertiser reported that "with a Spring tide the water will cover the tow-path under the railway bridge at Elm Road Crossing. A Neap tide does not come higher than 18in below the path and so is insufficient to keep the canal clean". The council also faced problems with residents dumping their rubbish and dead cats into the canal. (R.Fairhead)

53. Bare trees reflect in the icy waters of Wisbech Canal in this mid-1890s view of Elm Road, the first stopping place on the tramway. No. 125 is with Luggage Van no. 9 and six tramcars. Following the withdrawal of passenger services most of the tramcars were transferred to replace original stock on the Kelvedon & Tollesbury branch in Essex. On the canal bank Fenland Lightermen have unloaded a quantity of roadstone for resurfacing work. (The Boston Collection)

54. Luggage Van no. 9 was replaced in October 1903 by Brake Van no. 16. Built as a GER Brake 3rd in September 1875, this vehicle was converted into a full brake for use on the tramway. Seen here behind the tram engine, it was fitted with an end door and step plates for the guard's use. The locomotive is in the 1885/6 livery of brown woodwork, blue metalwork and 6in lettering. (B.Hilton coll.)

55. Driver Albert South observes the 8mph speed restriction as D2201 crosses Elm Road on Friday 20th May 1966. Signalman Harry Kidd appears to have bared his head in respect as cameramen record the last tram passing into history. (Lilian Ream Exhibition Gallery)

Tram-style tickets issued by the conductor-guard after departure from Wisbech.

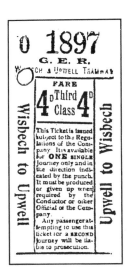

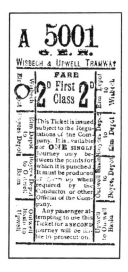

NEW COMMON BRIDGE

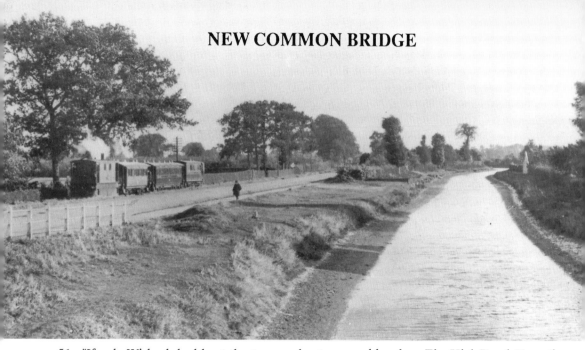

56. "If only Wisbech had kept the tram and canal" sigh local people; "it would have been a great tourist attraction." A solitary pedestrian walks towards New Common Bridge as the tram rumbles along Elm High Road. From the town's southern boundary, the canal route still marks the county boundary between Norfolk on the left and Cambridgeshire. (G.Drew coll.)

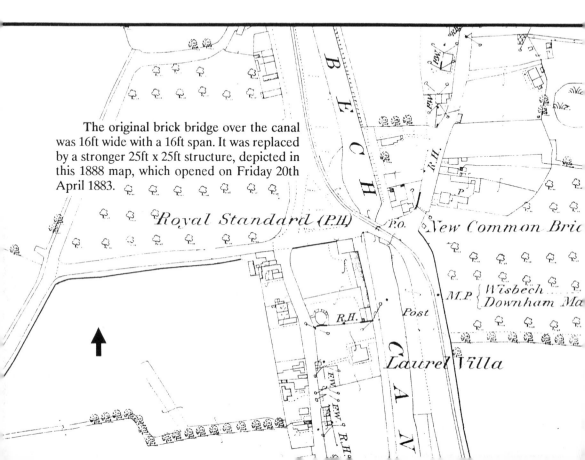

The original brick bridge over the canal was 16ft wide with a 16ft span. It was replaced by a stronger 25ft x 25ft structure, depicted in this 1888 map, which opened on Friday 20th April 1883.

Royal Standard (P.H.)

New Common Brid

Wisbech
Downham Ma

Laurel Villa

57. The second bridge was designed to carry the weight of road vehicles and the tramway, then under construction. On Saturday 31st December 1927, the last day of passenger services, an Upwell-bound tram crosses this hump-backed bridge. Robert Crofts of Elm took a sentimental journey on the last passenger tram, for as a baby of six weeks he had travelled on the inaugural run. He was still alive in 1983 when Wisbech celebrated the centenary of the line's opening. (National Railway Museum)

58. Old and new profiles are evident as work progresses on the third New Common Bridge in 1932. A concrete culvert with penstock gates will take the canal waters under Elm Road. Rail and road traffic still shared the same bridge, but the trams would no longer stall on the slippery gradient, whilst a wider carriageway ensured a trouble-free crossing for motorists. (Lilian Ream Exhibition Gallery)

59. Passenger traffic returned to the tramway on Sunday 9th September 1956 when the Railway Correspondence and Travel Society's "Fensman" railtour visited Wisbech. The 310 passengers left the comfort of their 10-coach train at Wisbech East to board fifteen open wagons and two brake vans for the journey to Upwell in a prolonged downpour of driving rain. (F.Hornby)

60. The author organised a Centenary Tram to mark the 100th anniversary of the tramway's opening. Departing from the site of Wisbech East at 9.30am on Saturday 20th August 1983, Tramcar no. 7 conveyed its original capacity of 32 passengers. The last time no. 7 travelled to Upwell was in 1927, the year in which Foster Showmans Engine no. 14589 was constructed. (Fenland Citizen)

BREWERY SIDING

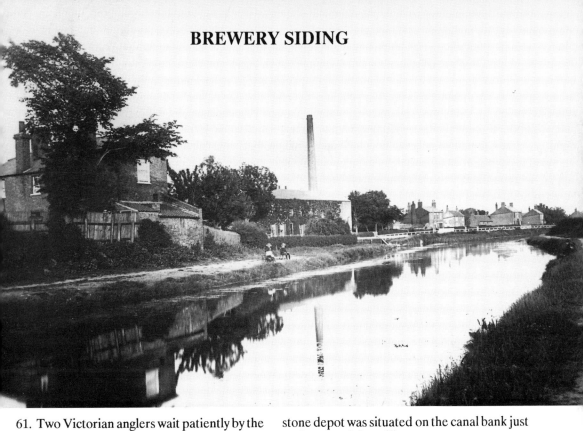

61. Two Victorian anglers wait patiently by the still waters of the Wisbech Canal. Flour gave way to hops by 1893 when the building became Fred Wood's Brewery. A second council road-stone depot was situated on the canal bank just to the east of the mill.
(Wisbech & Fenland Museum)

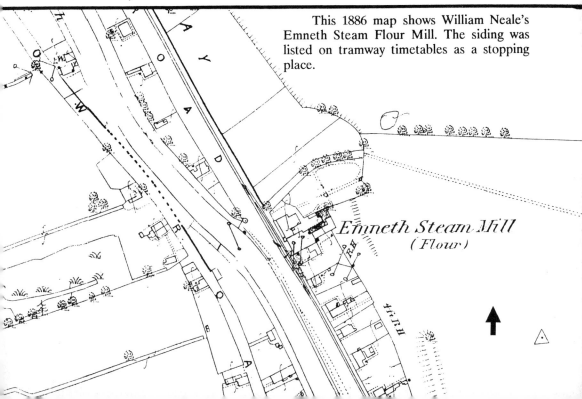

This 1886 map shows William Neale's Emneth Steam Flour Mill. The siding was listed on tramway timetables as a stopping place.

Emneth Steam Mill
(Flour)

62. The brewery was extensively damaged by fire which broke out soon after 1am on Wednesday 24th May 1911. Mr Percy Phillips, his wife and seven of their children escaped unhurt from the blaze, which was fuelled by spirits stored in the building. With firemen pumping water from the canal, the flames were eventually extinguished by 6am. (J.Mews coll.)

63. Following the fire, part of the mill was rebuilt as a private residence and the tramway siding lifted. Instead of this tranquil 1924 setting, the building now stands beside the busy A47 Wisbech by-pass roundabout. (Wisbech & Fenland Museum)

DUKE OF WELLINGTON
JUNCTION

64. Flanked by the Blacksmith's Arms and Duke of Wellington public houses, a Drewry shunter negotiates this accident blackspot. Cars travelling alongside the tram suddenly found the locomotive pulling out in front of them on this corner. (Stations U.K.)

The 1886 edition shows Elm Canal Bridge and two tram stopping places - Chapel Lane and the Duke of Wellington. Plans exist in Wisbech Museum for a branch from this point to the villages of Elm and Friday Bridge, but the line was never constructed.

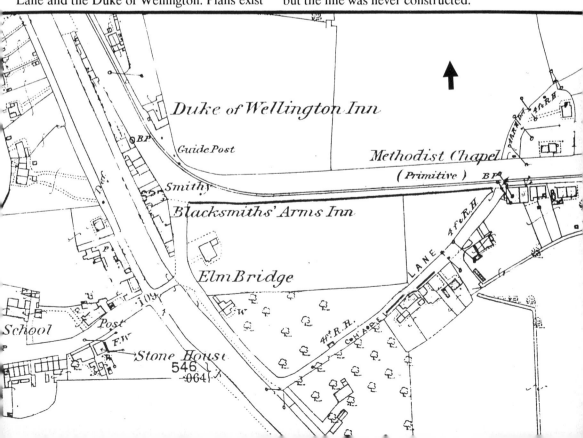

65. This is the view from the guards van as Drewry shunter no. 11102 crosses the road on Wednesday 4th June 1952, with the inaugural diesel tram to Upwell. An additional guards van was provided that day for 15 members of the Cambridge University Railway Club. Goods trams were often delayed on this stretch of line until vehicles parked outside the houses had been moved. (B.I.Nathan)

ELM CANAL BRIDGE

66. Ward's Cash Supply Stores is reflected in the still waters beside Elm Bridge in 1926. Each morning local residents would collect duck's eggs from the canal bank whilst their goats would feed along the towpath. Navigation on this stretch of waterway was abandoned with effect from Monday 14th June 1926. (Wisbech & Fenland Museum)

CHAPEL LANE

67. Two cyclists acknowledge J70 no. 7131 as it struggles towards Wisbech with loaded fruit vans on 2nd July 1946. Rev Teddy Boston remembered riding past St Ives station one lunchtime and almost falling off his bike in surprise, as the nearby gasworks hooter sounded exactly like a tram engine's whistle. (A.F.Cook)

68. On his standard gauge breakdown crane, Mr Brown is advertising a Day & Night service in the former Primitive Methodist Chapel. One Sunday, residents were woken by tramway staff at 2.30am and asked to move their cars for an Engineers train, sent to remove two lengths of rail at Upwell. (Lilian Ream Exhibition Gallery)

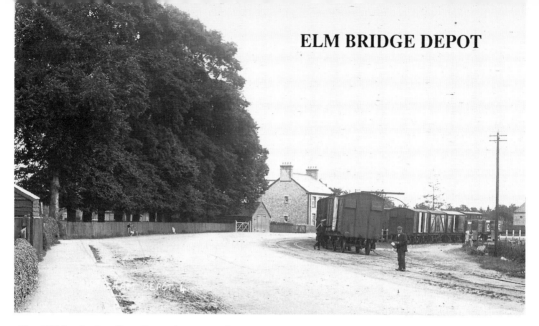

ELM BRIDGE DEPOT

69. Wisbech 2 miles, Downham Market 11 miles states the white milepost. Elm Bridge was one of three depots within the parish of Emneth, and this postcard, dated July 1915, emphasises the roadside nature of the tramway. Tommy Reeve was Depot Foreman at this time, in fact he held the post from 1884 to 1922. (J.H.Price coll.)

An 1886 map shows the first tram depot, 1 mile 53 chains from Wisbech Station. Elm Bridge Depot was situated some 500 yards east of Elm Canal Bridge.

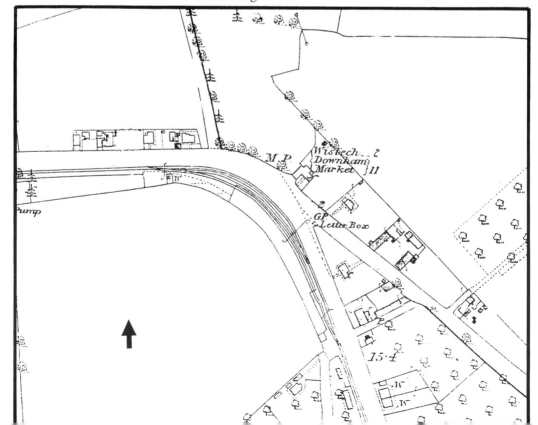

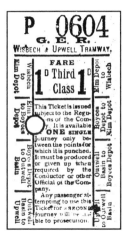
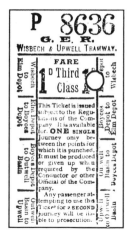

70. Every Goods Office on the tramway followed the same basic design: a 17ft 8in x 12ft 10in structure with a double door one end, two windows at the front, a single door at the far end, and a blank back wall. Daily takings were sent to Wisbech in a leather cash bag with the depot name stamped onto a brass plate. (J.Stafford-Baker/A.C.Ingram)

71. When completed in 1898 the waiting shed featured a glazed frontage, later replaced by an awning. The population of Emneth doubled during the trams passenger days from just 922 in 1891 to 1810 by 1921. The depot closed as from Monday 28th December 1964 but both buildings survived until 15th November 1978, when they were demolished by council workmen. (J.Stafford-Baker/A.C.Ingram)

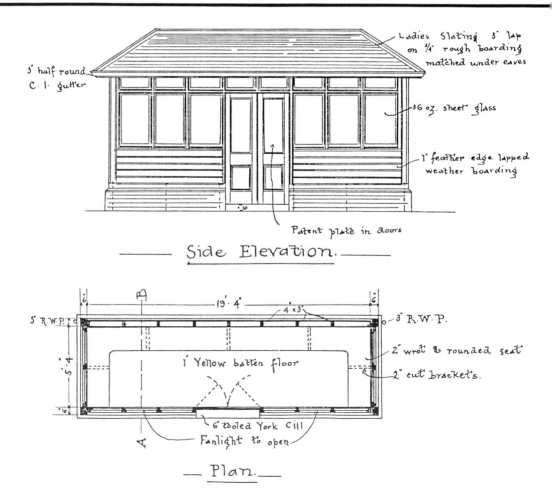

Ladies Slating 3" lap on 1/4" rough boarding matched under eaves

5" half round C. I. gutter

36 oz. sheet glass

1" feather edge lapped weather boarding

Patent plate in doors

Side Elevation.

19' 4"

4" x 3"

5" R.W.P.

3" R.W.P.

2" wrot & rounded seat

2" cut brackets.

1" Yellow batten floor

6" tooled York Cill

Fanlight to open.

Plan.

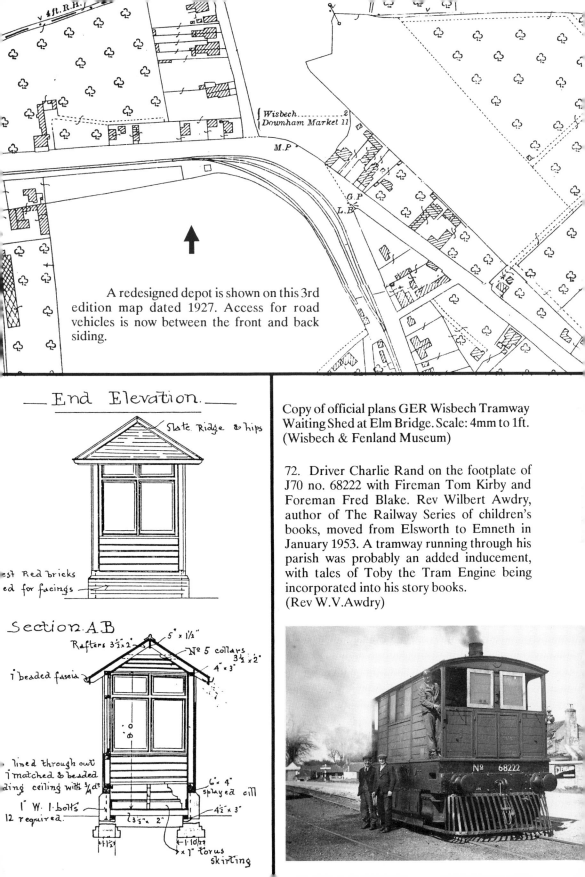

Wisbech........ 2
Downham Market 11

M.P

G.P

L.B

A redesigned depot is shown on this 3rd edition map dated 1927. Access for road vehicles is now between the front and back siding.

End Elevation.

Slate Ridge & hips

...st Red bricks
...ed for facings

Section AB

5" x 1½"
Rafters 3½" x 2"
№ 5 collars 3½" x 2"
4" x 3"
...i beaded fascia

lined through out
¼ matched & beaded
ding ceiling with ¾d"
1" W.I. bolts
12 required.
2½" x 2"
6" x 4" splayed cill
4½" x 3"
...1·10" x 1" torus skirting

Copy of official plans GER Wisbech Tramway Waiting Shed at Elm Bridge. Scale: 4mm to 1ft. (Wisbech & Fenland Museum)

72. Driver Charlie Rand on the footplate of J70 no. 68222 with Fireman Tom Kirby and Foreman Fred Blake. Rev Wilbert Awdry, author of The Railway Series of children's books, moved from Elsworth to Emneth in January 1953. A tramway running through his parish was probably an added inducement, with tales of Toby the Tram Engine being incorporated into his story books.
(Rev W.V. Awdry)

73. Coal was the main incoming traffic on the tramway with merchants based at Outwell Village and Upwell Depots. Private Owner wagons seen on the tramway included Austin & Co, Clay Cross, Coote & Warren, Dinnington, Dixons of Elm Bridge, Manchester Collieries, and Wigan Coal. (J.Stafford-Baker/A.C.Ingram)

British Railways Board (E)   BOOKING OFFICE
ISSUED AT .... WISBECH EAST ....   AB 067038

TO ...WISBECH EAST... (E)
FROM ...UPWELL TRAM DEPOT.. (E)   RETURN JOURNEY

Route ....
For alternative routes enquire at Booking Office.

DESCRIPTION		PASSENGERS NO. (in words)	FARE s. d.	AMOUNT £ s. d.	
ORDINARY FULL FARE	Adults	TWO	3 0	6 0	CLASS Second
	Children				
FORCES DUTY	Officers			— —	Valid —
	O/Ranks			— —	Outward ...†days/months
GROUP TRAVEL	Adults				Return...†days/months
	Children under 14				
	Young persons under 18				Commencing Date
Other Descriptions	Adults				16 Sept 1965 (Month in words)
	Children				
			Amount Paid	6 0	Warrant No.

NOT TRANSFERABLE

Issued subject to The Conditions and Regulations in the Board's Publications and Notices.   BR 4404/1

INGLETHORPE HALL

74. Behind the trees stands Inglethorpe Hall, formerly the home of Squire Francis Maltby Bland JP. His gardener erected nesting boxes for squirrels who would leap across the tramway to another line of trees, felled in 1933 to make way for the bungalows. D2201 encounters no such flying hazards as it passes the site on 27th September 1965. Rev Boston, who had left Wisbech ten years earlier, referred to this type of motive power as the infernal combustion engine.(Rev W.V.Awdry)

This Ticket is issued subject to Regulations of the Company. It is available for a single journey only and must be produced on demand of the Conductor or other Official of the Company & given up on leaving the Car. Any passenger attempting to use this Ticket for a second journey will be liable to prosecution

Brass-rubbing of 9in x 5in worksplate on Y6 no. 7134. Made direct from the locomotive at Wisbech Tram Shed.

COLLETTS BRIDGE

75. Built in 1797 at a cost of £226, there were holes in the roadway through which school children might fall by 1931. It was therefore demolished and replaced by a girder bridge at a total cost of £250, opening for traffic on Friday 4th December 1931.
(Wisbech & Fenland Museum)

Originally called Gosmere Bridge, and known by the locals as Collett's Bridge, this 1886 map describes it as Emneth Bridge.

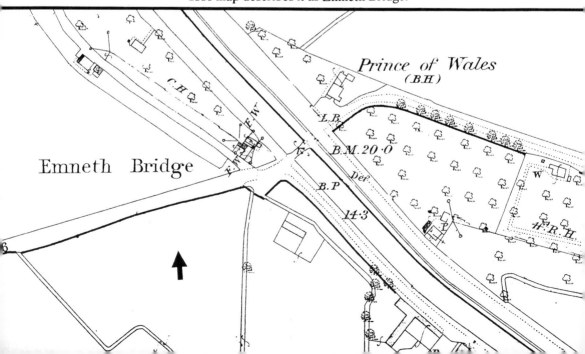

76. Drivers mate Henry Hulme was tragically killed on Thursday 20th April 1933 when the steering failed on his cattle lorry. Guided by the tram rails the vehicle travelled for 28 yards towards Wisbech before somersaulting into the canal. Driver Kenneth Johnson and all five cattle managed to escape from the wreckage. (Lilian Ream Exhibition Gallery)

SHEPHERD'S COTTAGE

77. Class J70 no. 7130 passing Shepherd's Cottage on Tuesday 2nd July 1946, during the height of the fruit season. Rev Boston's illustrated talks about his travels on the tramway were full of anecdotes. He recalled one exhilarating 35mph footplate ride on a strawberry special, almost three times the permitted speed limit. Wilbert Awdry and Teddy Boston later appeared as themselves in The Railway Series of children's books, as The Thin Clergyman and The Fat Clergyman. (A.F.Cook)

BOYCE'S BRIDGE DEPOT

78. Humphrey Household travelled from York to Wisbech in December 1927 to photograph the last day of passenger services on the tramway. Here he had persuaded the drivers to wait while he took a photograph of goods and passenger trams passing at Boyce's Bridge. A similar request to staff on an InterCity express may not be so well received. (National Railway Museum)

The 1886 edition showing Boyce's Bridge Depot, which at 3 miles 25 chains from Wisbech, was regarded as the half-way point along the tramway.

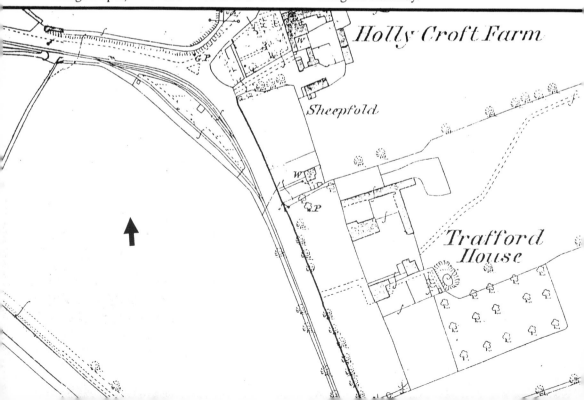

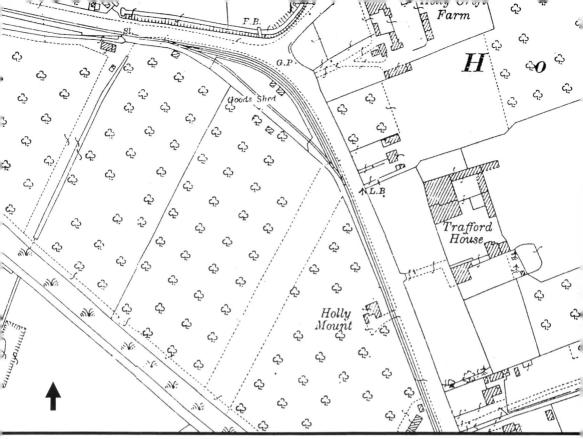

This 1927 3rd edition shows the extended
passing loop alongside Bird's Corner.

79. The driver, conductor and one passenger all escaped without injury when their Eastern Counties bus plunged into a dyke opposite Boyce's Bridge Depot at 1.15pm on Sunday 22nd April 1934. The accident was caused, according to the local paper, by two buses travelling in opposite directions reaching the corner at the same time.
(Lilian Ream Exhibition Gallery)

80. No. 11102 stands beside the goods office with the afternoon tram from Wisbech on 27th March 1957. The foreman was responsible for unlocking the points to allow access to the passing loop and back siding. Even though the Drewry diesels had been fitted with double aspect electric marker lights, staff were obliged to use oil lamps. (W.J.Naunton)

81. No. 11102 leaves most of its train on the main line and collects two loaded vans from the siding. Rev Awdry left the parish of Emneth in 1965 for active retirement in Gloucestershire. The last story book in The Railway Series to be written by him, *Tramway Engines,* introduced readers to *Mavis* the diesel shunter. (W.J.Naunton)

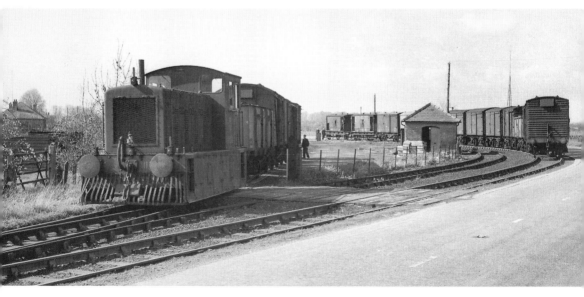

82. Following the closure of Boyce's Bridge Depot on Monday 5th November 1962, road improvements were proposed to ease Birds Corner. In December 1963 work was under way to lift the main and loop lines, leaving the tram to traverse the gated back siding for its final three years. The look-out man seems dejected with little opportunity to wave his flags. (Rev W.V.Awdry)

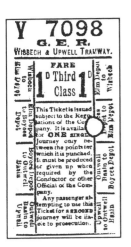

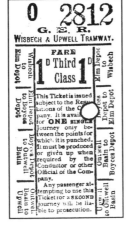

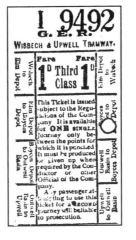

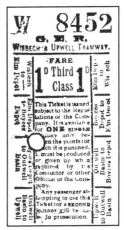

DIAL HOUSE

83. No. D2201 with the final tram from Upwell leaves a 440 yard stretch of reserved track and approaches Dial House. In the foreground a tidal wave of landfill had erased the canal from the landscape. A road was laid on the canal route between Shepherd's Cottage and Outwell Basin in 1989.
(Lilian Ream Exhibition Gallery)

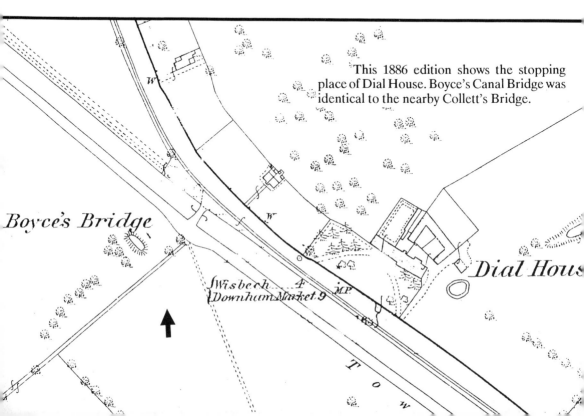

This 1886 edition shows the stopping place of Dial House. Boyce's Canal Bridge was identical to the nearby Collett's Bridge.

Boyce's Bridge

Wisbech 4
Downham Market 9   MP

Dial Hous

T O
W

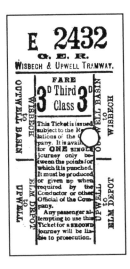
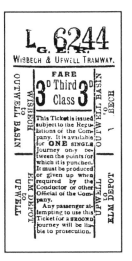
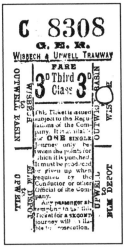

84. Police with tracker dogs search for clues along the tramway following the brutal killing of local fruitgrower John Auger on Friday 10th March 1967. His farmhouse had contained one of the largest and most valuable private collections of porcelain in the country. Superintendent Virgo of Scotland Yard led the investigation which resulted in the arrest and conviction for manslaughter of three men. (Lilian Ream Exhibition Gallery)

OUTWELL BASIN DEPOT

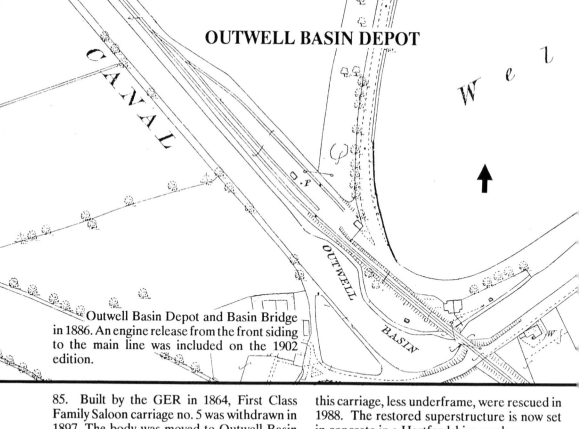

Outwell Basin Depot and Basin Bridge in 1886. An engine release from the front siding to the main line was included on the 1902 edition.

85. Built by the GER in 1864, First Class Family Saloon carriage no. 5 was withdrawn in 1897. The body was moved to Outwell Basin where it served as a passenger waiting room and then a store shed. The skeletal remains of this carriage, less underframe, were rescued in 1988. The restored superstructure is now set in concrete in a Hertfordshire garden. (J.Stafford-Baker/A.C.Ingram)

86. Drewry diesel mechanical shunter no. D2201 entered service on the tramway in August 1952. Apart from a months loan to Plaistow depot in March 1955, it remained on the line until closure, being transferred from March to Crewe Works on 15th September 1966. Withdrawn from service on 6th April 1968, it was sold to a scrap merchant in Yorkshire. (J.Stafford-Baker/A.C.Ingram)

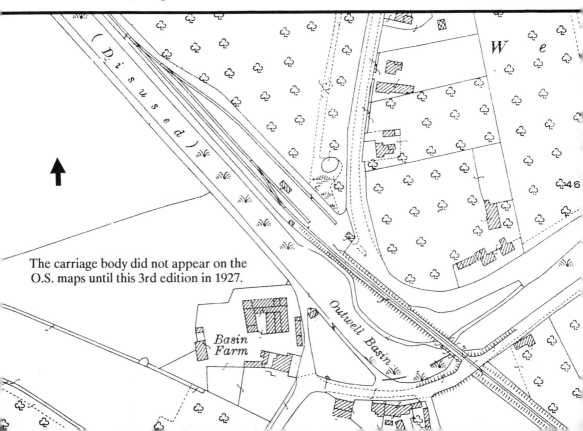

The carriage body did not appear on the O.S. maps until this 3rd edition in 1927.

87. This is a general view of the tramway's 1883 terminus, ten years after its closure on 5th October 1964. The depot and its carriage were featured in two Anglia Television documentaries during the 1983 Centenary celebrations. The foreground is now the site of a roundabout. (A.C.Ingram)

YOUR REF.		BRITISH RAILWAYS	OUR REF. S.M. Pad	B.R. 3/6
DATED			DATE 9.10.63	

TO   Mr Newman
     Outwell Basin

FROM   Station Master
       Wisbech East

(Centre No.   )   Extn............   (Centre No.   )

Rationalisation of Facilities Upwell Tramway

Outwell Basin will be closed after Friday Oct. 11th. Will you please advise your regular loaders.

You should return to your normal duties at Wisbech East Harbour from Monday Oct. 14th.

BASIN BRIDGE

88. A canal basin was excavated beside the depot for the berthing and turning of craft. To allow clearance for navigation, the tramway climbed a steep 1 in 30 gradient to reach Basin Bridge. With a standing start from the depot drivers with heavy loads sometimes had to set back then open the regulator wide to get over the bridge. (J.Stafford-Baker/A.C.Ingram)

89. An unusual feature of the bridge were gates at the Outwell end, possibly to prevent motorists or cattle on the adjacent minor road taking a wrong turning or short-cut. The ornate cast iron posts have been incorporated into a nearby garden fence.
(J.Stafford-Baker/A.C.Ingram)

90. No. D2201 has descended the embankment and traverses the 660 yards of reserved track between Basin Bridge and Horn's Corner. This route avoided the tortuous bends taken by the road and canal on their approach to Outwell. (J.Stafford-Baker/A.C.Ingram)

SCOTT'S BRIDGE

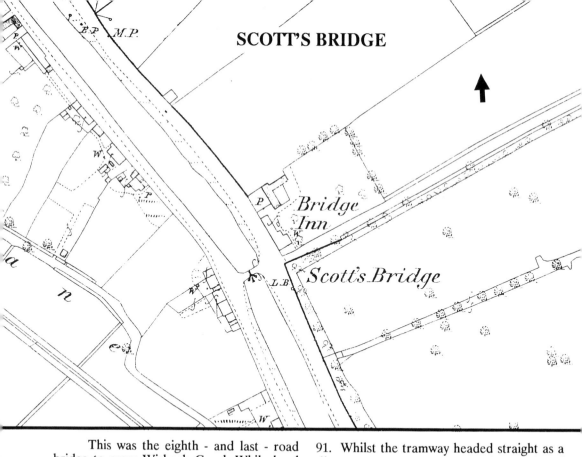

This was the eighth - and last - road bridge to cross Wisbech Canal. While local residents have always known it as Gill's Bridge, this 1886 Ordnance Survey map and the 1981 Landranger edition continue to name it Scott's Bridge.

91. Whilst the tramway headed straight as a die across country, the canal meandered towards Outwell. The Bridge Inn stands beside Scotts Bridge in 1926, the year in which navigation on the Wisbech Canal was finally abandoned. (Wisbech & Fenland Museum)

	WEEK DAYS.							NS	SO
	morn	morn	morn	even.	even.	even.	even.	even.	even.
UPWELL ....dep.	8 15	10 15	11 40	1 25	3 15	5 15	7 5	9 15	9 45
Outwell Village — „	8 21	10 21	11 46	1 31	3 21	5 21	7 11	9 21	9 51
Outwell Basin......... „	8 27	10 27	11 52	1 37	3 27	5 27	7 17	9 27	9 57
Boyce's Depot— — „	8 33	10 33	11 58	1 43	3 33	5 33	7 23	9 33	10 3
Elm Depot............... „	8 43	10 43	12 8	1 53	3 43	5 43	7 33	9 43	10 13
WISBECH — —arr.	8 54	10 54	12 19	2 4	3 54	5 54	7 44	9 54	10 24

NS Not Saturdays.   **SO** Saturdays only.

January 1923

92. In 1927 the Norfolk and Isle of Ely County Councils jointly funded the rebuilding of Scott's Bridge, which crossed their boundary. The new bridge was extended to 30ft wide, the crown was lowered by 3ft, whilst the canal waters were piped through a 4ft concrete culvert. Note the new penstock gate lying amid the reeds. (Lilian Ream Exhibition Gallery)

HORN'S CORNER

93. When approaching the corner tram drivers were always extra careful if they saw a horse prick up its ears. Local fruitgrower Bobby Allen (65) was killed when his pony suddenly backed and shot the lorry's front end into the oncoming 3.30pm tram from Upwell on Wednesday 6th July 1932. Mr Allen had been returning home after taking his load of strawberries to Outwell Basin, thus avoiding a long wait at the overcrowded Outwell Village Depot. (Lilian Ream Exhibition Gallery)

94. This is the driver's view of Horn's Corner from the cab of D2201 on the return journey to Wisbech. The cottage beyond the crossing was designed and built by the Great Eastern Railway for their Goods Foreman at Outwell Village Depot. The original plans, dated 14th August 1914, are now in the Wisbech & Fenland Museum.
(J.Stafford-Baker/A.C.Ingram)

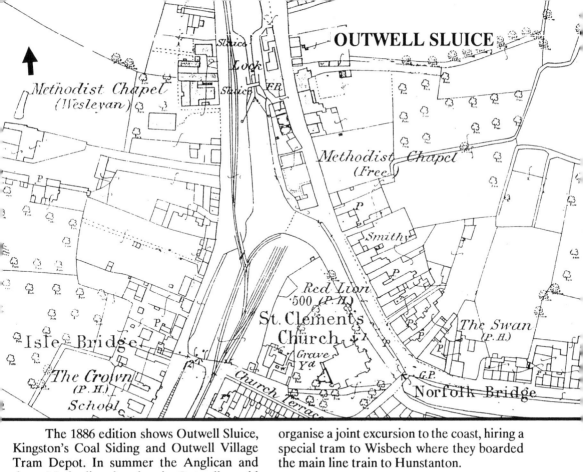

OUTWELL SLUICE

Methodist Chapel
(Wesleyan)

Sluice
Lock
Sluice
F.B.

Methodist Chapel
(Free)

Smithy

Red Lion
·500 (P.H.)

St. Clements
Church

The Swan
(P.H.)

Isle Bridge

Grave
Yd

The Crown
(P.H.)

School

Church Terrace

G.P.

Norfolk Bridge

The 1886 edition shows Outwell Sluice, Kingston's Coal Siding and Outwell Village Tram Depot. In summer the Anglican and three Methodist churches in Outwell would organise a joint excursion to the coast, hiring a special tram to Wisbech where they boarded the main line train to Hunstanton.

95. The final stretch of the canal is seen here in 1929, with St Clement's Church in the distance. In 1931 the ecclesiastical parish population was 1378, an increase of almost 200 since the census of 1911. The rake of wagons on the right are stabled in William Kingston's coal siding. (Lilian Ream Exhibition Gallery)

96. The first tolls were collected at Outwell Sluice on 9th January 1796, with the 1851 census naming John Pacey as sluice keeper. By 1995, the sluice keeper's cottage (behind the bush), three paddle-posts and stone edging were the only physical remains of the canal at Outwell. (Cambridgeshire Collection, Cambridgeshire Libraries)

Outwell Sluice Toll Receipts						
	£	s	d		£	s	d
1796	341	15	0	1865	416	4	0
1800	497	3	11	1870	387	7	6
1805	660	4	6	1875	203	2	9
1810	452	10	3	1880	227	8	2
1815	784	6	7	1885	151	6	9
1820	301	4	1	1890	171	13	8
1825	328	16	0	1895	56	10	6
1830	142	19	2	1900	75	0	5
1835	187	17	9	1905	11	18	3
1840	337	19	10	1910	23	4	1
1845	758	6	8	1915	13	16	9
1850	227	6	9	1920		17	6
1855	350	7	6	1922		12	6
1860	417	15	10				

97. The 97ft lock at Outwell was photographed in 1929. A tale is told of Henry Bond who was being chased by Henry Hartley, a bill poster of Upwell. Bond evaded capture by leaping across the 11ft 6in wide sluice. Children standing on the sluice bridge may be waiting for a repeat performance. (Lilian Ream Exhibition Gallery)

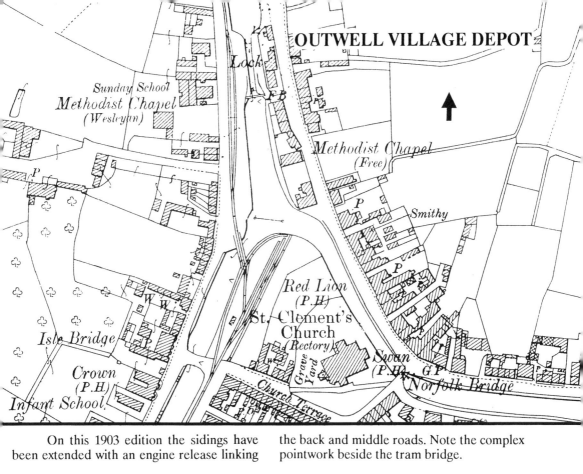

OUTWELL VILLAGE DEPOT

On this 1903 edition the sidings have been extended with an engine release linking the back and middle roads. Note the complex pointwork beside the tram bridge.

98. The year is 1887 and builders are carrying out repairs to St. Clement's Church, and installing a new chiming clock to mark Queen Victoria's Golden Jubilee. This view, just three years after the depot opened, includes two GER 5-plank wagons fitted with wooden brake blocks on split-spoked wheels. (Lilian Ream Exhibition Gallery)

99. The picturesque setting of Outwell Village Depot has made it a popular choice amongst railway modellers. A member of staff moves to protect the ungated Church Terrace crossing as G15 0-4-0T no. 126 leaves for Upwell.

Following pressure from the Well Creek Trust, the goods office was granted a Grade II preservation order in October 1990. (Lens of Sutton)

GREAT EASTERN RAILWAY.
WISBECH & OUTWELL TRAMWAYS

J 3492

FARE   FARE
3d **SECOND 3**d
CLASS.

This Ticket is issued s...
to the **Regulations** of the Company. It is **available** for a
SINGLE journey only—on the
Car where issued. It must be
produced on demand of the
Conductor or other Official of
the Company, and **given up**
on leaving the Car. Any passenger attempting to use this
Ticket for a **SECOND** journey,
will be liable to **Prosecution.**

An early ticket with the optimistic title WISBECH & OUTWELL TRAMWAYS. The GER abolished Second Class on 1st January 1893. (D.Geldard coll.)

G. E. R.

WISBECH HORSE SHOW

WEDNESDAY, 2nd *JULY,* 1913,

RETURN TICKETS

AT A

Single Fare and a **Third**

(no less charge than 1s. for an Adult Passenger)

WILL BE ISSUED TO

WISBECH

by any train, from Peterboro', King's Lynn, St. Ives,
Cambridge, Ely, and Intermediate Stations; also
from Godmanchester, Ramsey, Warboys, Somersham,
Chatteris, Wimblington, Spalding, and Intermediate
Stations (G.N. & G.E. Joint Line), available for return
the same day, by any train.

Fractional parts of a penny are charged as one penny.

Children under 3 years of age, free; above 3 and under 12, half-price. No luggage allowed.

A SPECIAL TRAM CAR
WILL LEAVE

AT **WISBECH**
p.m.
FOR

11.15 UPWELL

London, May, 1913.   WALTER H. HYDE, General Manager.
1/4700   Printed at the Company's Works, Stratford.   43605.

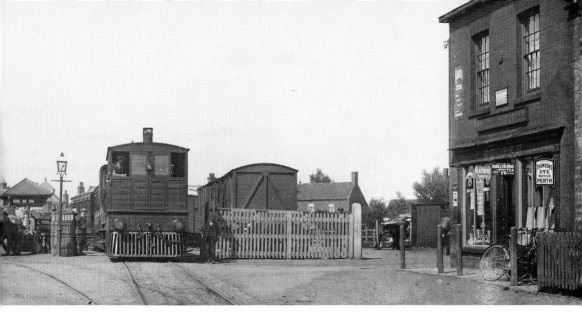

100.   Outwell Village is probably the most photographed depot on the tramway, yet this is the first view to include the waiting room. Situated to the left of the lamp-post, it was built to the same design as Elm Bridge. No. 127 had the shortest lifespan of any 0-4-0T tram. Built in January 1892, it was withdrawn just 22 years later in December 1913. A special Saturday late tram was introduced in 1910, leaving Wisbech at 9.30pm which would have been greatly appreciated by those who come from the villages to Wisbech to do their shopping, or in search of pleasure. (B.Hilton coll.)

101.   Many farms in The Fens were only accessible by water until well into the twentieth century. In 1909 about 40 pumping stations were still receiving their coal supplies by Fenland Lighter from Outwell Depot. The weed-covered siding (right) and reeds by the chute (numbered 2 and standing vertically) suggest that coal has not been transferred from wagon to waterway for some time. The photograph was taken on 28th June 1950. (A.C.Ingram coll.)

102. Driver Charlie Rand says goodbye to Ernie Gretton, who was retiring on Saturday 13th August 1960 after 30 years as foreman at Outwell Village Depot. Fireman Edward Nichols is also on the footplate of no. 11101 with Charlie Barton (the new Foreman). Guard Arthur Blake holds the shunting pole. (Lilian Ream Exhibition Gallery)

103. The original livery for this locomotive was unlined black with red bufferbeams. In December 1961 no. 11101 became D2201 with a revised livery of unlined green with yellow and black warning stripes. On the footplate is David Bailey who joined the tramway staff in 1956 and found this to be the stronger of the two regular Drewry shunters.
(Dr I.C.Allen/C.Moss)

104. Charles Scott JP, who opened Outwell's Summer Fair on Saturday 19th June 1965, prepares to go for a ride with some youngsters on a permanent way trolley. The newspaper stated "that a feature of the Fair was a tramcar race to Goodman's Crossing." Previous un-official excursions to Upwell on this trolley had been hotly pursued by the village bobby on his bicycle. The depot remained open for goods traffic until the line closed in 1966.
(Lilian Ream Exhibition Gallery)

105. The guard leans out of his van as the 3.20pm tram from Upwell cautiously approaches the ungated level crossing on 7th June 1950. Note the point lever on the roadside which controlled access to the water road. This bridge keystone is dated 1852, whereas the corresponding stone on the opposite side states 1682.(M.N.Bland)

106. Following its withdrawal in October 1951, tramcar no. 7 served as an onion shed near Huntingdon for over 20 years before it was discovered and purchased for preservation. On loan from the Rutland Railway Museum at Cottesmore, no. 7 crosses Tuck's Bridge with the Centenary Tram on Saturday 20th August 1983. As it was running to the original timetable this was the first opportunity for holiday traffic to overtake since New Common Bridge was passed 45 minutes earlier! (John Day Photographers)

107. Well Creek sweeps past Outwell Village Depot and the silted-up entrance to Wisbech Canal in this August 1955 photograph. The Creek also fell into disuse, but was reopened for navigation on 1st June 1975 by the Middle Level commissioners with the support of Well Creek Trust and the Inland Waterways Association. The Trust now manage this eight-mile canalised river between Marmont Priory and Salter's Lode. (Aerofilms)

GOODMAN'S CROSSING

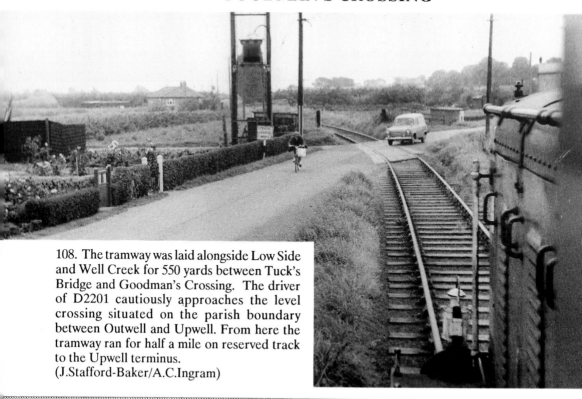

108. The tramway was laid alongside Low Side and Well Creek for 550 yards between Tuck's Bridge and Goodman's Crossing. The driver of D2201 cautiously approaches the level crossing situated on the parish boundary between Outwell and Upwell. From here the tramway ran for half a mile on reserved track to the Upwell terminus.
(J.Stafford-Baker/A.C.Ingram)

SMALL LODE

109. While pupils and staff from the nearby Upwell School enjoy their summer holidays, tramway staff pause at Small Lode crossing with the 12.45pm from Wisbech on Friday 25th August 1950. Driver Albert South stands beside J70 no. 68217, with Fireman Arthur Banyard and Richard Casserley, the photographer's son, on the footplate.
(H.C.Casserley)

WISBECH & UPWELL
TRAMWAY.

TIME TABLE
2nd OCTOBER, 1922, and until further notice.
WEEK-DAYS.

		MONDAYS TO FRIDAYS INCLUSIVE.							SATURDAYS ONLY.						
		a.m.	a.m.	a.m.	p.m.	p.m.	p.m.	p.m.	a.m.	a.m.	a.m.	p.m.	p.m.	p.m.	p.m.
Wisbech Station	dep.	7 52	9 30	10 55	12 40	2 45	5 32	8 0	7 52	9 30	11 55	3 5	5 32	7 20	9 0
Elm Depot		8 3	9 41	11 6	12 51	2 56	5 43	8 11	8 3	9 41	12 6	3 16	5 43	7 31	9 11
Boyce's Depot		8 13	9 51	11 16	1 1	3 6	5 53	8 21	8 13	9 51	12 16	3 26	5 53	7 37	9 21
Outwell Basin		8 19	9 57	11 22	1 7	3 12	5 59	8 27	8 19	9 57	12 22	3 32	5 59	7 47	9 27
Outwell Village		8 25	10 3	11 28	1 13	3 18	6 5	8 33	8 25	10 3	12 28	3 38	6 5	7 53	9 33
Upwell	arr.	8 31	10 9	11 34	1 19	3 24	6 11	8 39	8 31	10 9	12 34	3 44	6 11	7 59	9 39
		a.m.	a.m.	a.m.	p.m.	p.m.	p.m.	p.m.	a.m.	a.m.	a.m.	p.m.	p.m.	p.m.	p.m.
Upwell	dep.	8 35	10 15	11 40	1 25	3 32	6 16	8 50	8 35	10 15	1 3	4 6	6 16	8 5	9 45
Outwell Village		8 41	10 21	11 46	1 31	3 38	6 22	8 56	8 41	10 21	1 9	4 12	6 22	8 11	9 51
Outwell Basin		8 47	10 27	11 52	1 37	3 44	6 28	9 2	8 47	10 27	1 15	4 18	6 28	8 17	9 57
Boyce's Depot		8 53	10 33	11 58	1 43	3 50	6 34	9 8	8 53	10 33	1 21	4 24	6 34	8 23	10 3
Elm Depot		9 3	10 43	12 8	1 53	4 6	6 44	9 18	9 3	10 43	1 31	4 34	6 44	8 33	10 13
Wisbech Station	arr.	9 14	10 54	12 19	2 4	4 11	6 55	9 29	9 14	10 54	1 42	4 45	6 55	8 44	10 24

In addition to the above stopping places, the tram cars will also stop at the following points if required, for the purpose of taking up or setting down passengers, viz:—Elm Road Crossing, New Common Bridge (Canal Bridge), Rose Cottage, Duke of Wellington Junction, Inglethorpe Hall, Collett's Bridge, Shepherd's Cottage, Dial House, Basin Gate, Horn's Corner, Goodman's Crossing and Small Lode. The tram cars will not stop at any other point along the line of route.

FARES.

	Wisbech. 1st Class 3rd Class	Elm Depot. 1st Class 3rd Class	Boyce's Depot. 1st Class 3rd Class	Outwell Basin. 1st Class 3rd Class	Outwell Village 1st Class 3rd Class	Upwell.
Elm Depot	3½d. 2d.					
Boyce's Depot	5½d. 3½d.	3d. 2d.				
Outwell Basin	9d. 5d.	5d. 3½d.	3½d. 2d.			
Outwell Village	10½d. 7d.	9d. 5d.	5d. 3½d.	3½d. 2d.		
Upwell	10½d. 7d.	9d. 5d.	5d. 3½d.	3½d. 2d.	3½d. 2d.	

Personal luggage not exceeding 28 lbs. in weight will be allowed to be taken by each adult passenger free of charge if carried by hand.

RETURN MARKET TICKETS are issued to WISBECH on Thursdays and Saturdays as under:—

FROM				Return Market fare.	
Upwell		...	...	10d.	
Outwell Village		...	...	10d.	Third Class.
Outwell Basin		...	...	8d.	

By cars leaving Upwell at 8.35, 10.15, 11.40 (Thursdays only) a.m., 1.3 (Saturdays only) p.m., and 1.25 (Thursdays only) p.m.

The tickets are issued at a reduced rate and subject to the condition that the Company shall not be liable for any loss, damage, injury or delay to passengers arising from any cause.

MERCHANDISE TRAFFIC
is dealt with at the following Sidings or Depots:—
ELM DEPOT, BOYCE'S DEPOT, OUTWELL BASIN, OUTWELL VILLAGE, AND UPWELL.

The charges for haulage are very moderate; particulars of these and other information can be obtained from the Company's Inspectors at the Depots, from the Station Agent at Wisbech, the Divisional Commercial Superintendent at Cambridge, or the Commercial Superintendent at Liverpool Street.

London, Sept., 1922.

7258/H/22—150   No. 41.   Printed at the Company's Works, Stratford.

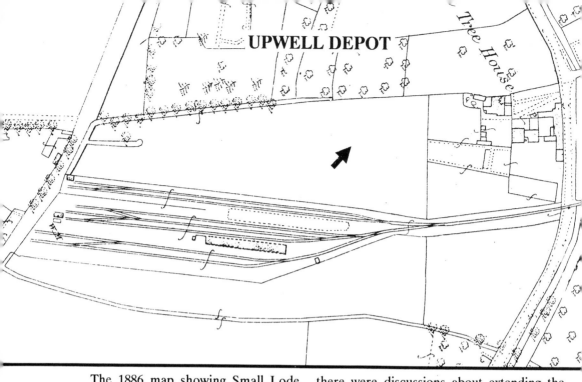

UPWELL DEPOT

The 1886 map showing Small Lode (right), the last stopping place on the tramway, and Upwell Depot. When the tramway opened there were discussions about extending the line from Upwell to Lakesend and Welney.

110. A passenger tram from Wisbech stands beside the waiting room at Upwell. On Thursday 26th December 1901, an elderly passenger attempting to board a moving tram slipped and fell under the wheels as it left the depot. His body was placed in the waiting room, where it lay until after the inquest at Upwell the following week. (Cambridgeshire Collection, Cambridgeshire Libraries)

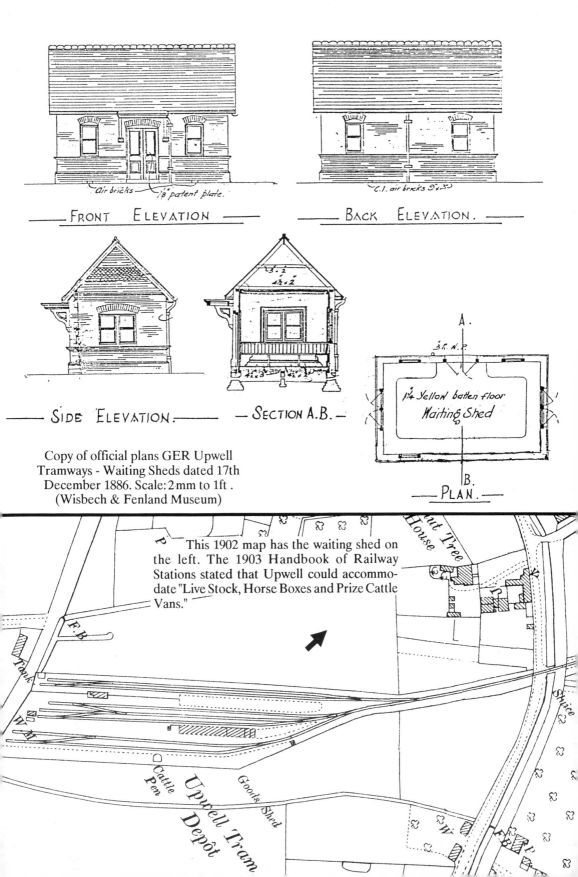

— FRONT ELEVATION — — BACK ELEVATION. —

air bricks — ⅛ patent plate.   C.I. air bricks 9"×3"

— SIDE ELEVATION.— — SECTION A.B. —

Copy of official plans GER Upwell
Tramways - Waiting Sheds dated 17th
December 1886. Scale: 2 mm to 1 ft .
(Wisbech & Fenland Museum)

A.

3.r. N.P.

1¼ Yellow batten floor
Waiting Shed

B.
— PLAN. —

This 1902 map has the waiting shed on
the left. The 1903 Handbook of Railway
Stations stated that Upwell could accommo-
date "Live Stock, Horse Boxes and Prize Cattle
Vans."

111. A class J70 pilots class Y1 Sentinel no. 8401 as they prepare to leave Upwell with a passenger tram on 4th May 1927. This photograph shows for the first time not only a double-headed tram, but also a J70 on passenger duties. No. 8401 was returned to the Lowestoft Civil Engineers Department following these trials. It had a vertical boiler on the right and a vertical engine in the middle of the body, with chain drive to each axle. (R.H.R.Garraway)

112. Here is a panoramic view from the depot throat in 1937, with the former passenger roads on the right and several stacks of apple barrels. In the 1931 census for Upwell there were 1918 residents on the Norfolk side with another 1621 across Well Creek in Cambridgeshire. The foreman at this time was Wilson Peacock, and his cottage with its tall chimney was still occupied in 1995. (National Railway Museum)

113. The photographer carefully positioned the tramway staff then set the delayed action shutter for this 1937 portrait. Seconds later the barrels gave way under their weight! Front row: Albert Blake, Joe Swaine, Albert Helstrip, Wilson Peacock, Bill Sizeland. Middle row: Jack Ogden, Fred Cole, Fred Paget. Top row: Harry Ellis, Arthur Godfrey, Al Fysh. (H.G.Ellis)

114. During the summer Fruit Traffic Office Vans would be brought into service. Starting at Wisbech they dropped one clerk at each depot to Upwell, where two remained. They waybilled as much traffic as possible before the van returned to collect them up en route to Wisbech. Consignment notes not dealt with were then waybilled in the Office Van before arrival at Wisbech, where the waybills were attached to the fruit vans as they arrived. Van no. 962353, originally built as a GER Sundry Van in October 1897, was converted to a FTOV around 1937 and withdrawn circa 1950. (A.F.Cook)

115. Thursday was cattle market day in
Wisbech and many cattle trucks would be
attached to the early morning goods tram. In
the late afternoon the trucks would return with
calves and heifers bought by farmers for
fattening. No. 68222 stands beside the sidings
and pens in 1950, now silent and covered with
weeds. (H.C.Casserley)

116. The water tower at Upwell consisted of a
former Great Eastern locomotive tender on a
wooden trestle. On the original plans for the
foremans cottage, dated 3rd July 1901, this
tank and the cottage were connected by a 1in
galvanised iron pipe. The photograph was
taken during a Cambridge University Railway
Club visit on Wednesday 7th June 1950.
(M.N.Bland)

117. In BR days the sidings had no engine release, therefore it had to get free by a fly shunt. David Bailey recalled "you'd approach the yard at a fair good speed, ease up as the shunter snapped the coupling off, then go like the clappers. As you accelerated past the junction, the points were changed so that the engine went into one road and the wagons into another." No. 11102 tried this but the speed governor automatically applied the brakes and the wagons hit her hard. *The Fat Controller steps across the track to speak with Mavis whilst Toby chuckles behind a bush. He knew that she could have used the engine release on the passenger side.* (B.I.Nathan)

118. Following the introduction of Drewry diesel shunters in June 1952, J70 nos. 68217/68222/68223/68225 were stored at March shed. No. 68222 briefly returned to the Tramway in 1953 after both diesels had failed. It arrived at Upwell only to discover that the water tower had been removed, rendering the water column useless. Rev Awdry watches the 625 gallon tank being filled using a garden hose borrowed from the local vicarage. His son Christopher took the photograph, and thirty years later began writing stories for his father's Railway Series. (C.V.Awdry)

119. A lifeless water column stands beside the cold ashpit on Sunday 20th March 1960. The fruit vans in the background were sometimes used by tramps as a night shelter. Tramway staff were alerted the following morning by angry shouts from within after local youngsters had slammed the van doors shut. On another occasion Foreman Mike Francis opened a van door to discover the vehicle laden with American cigarettes and Scotch Whisky. (J.H.Price/A.C.Ingram)

120. Snow settles on Upwell Depot and the tramway's future prospects look bleak. Boyce's Bridge Depot had closed in 1962 whilst facilities at Elm Bridge and Outwell Basin were withdrawn in 1964. Upwell Depot closed on 23rd May 1966, and by April 1974 this site had been cleared to make way for Townley Close housing estate and Upwell Health Centre. (J.Stafford-Baker/A.C.Ingram)

121. The closing scene in "The Railway Children" film comes to mind in this view of the Centenary Tram standing on the site of Upwell Depot in 1983. The Mayor of Wisbech (Beryl Petts), Drivers Albert South and Charlie Rand, and author Christopher Awdry join other invited guests in celebrating this unique and friendly line.
(Peterborough Evening Telegraph)

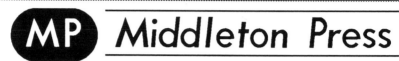

Easebourne Lane, Midhurst. West Sussex. GU29 9AZ   Tel: 01730 813169 Fax: 01730 812601

..... *Write or telephone for our latest list* .....

BRANCH LINES

Branch Line to Allhallows
Branch Lines to Alton
Branch Lines around Ascot
Branch Line to Bude
Branch Lines around Canterbury
Branch Lines to East Grinstead
Branch Lines around Effingham Jn
Branch Lines to Exmouth
Branch Line to Fairford
Branch Line to Hawkhurst
Branch Lines to Horsham
Branch Lines around Huntingdon
Branch Lines to Ilfracombe
Branch Line to Lyme Regis
Branch Line to Lynton
Branch Lines around March
Branch Lines around Midhurst
Branch Lines to Newport
Branch Line to Padstow
Branch Lines around Portmadoc 1923-46
Branch Lines around Porthmadog 1954-94
Branch Lines to Seaton & Sidmouth
Branch Line to Selsey
Branch Lines around Sheerness
Branch Line to Southwold
Branch Line to Swanage
Branch Line to Tenterden
Branch Lines to Torrington
Branch Lines to Tunbridge Wells
Branch Lines around Weymouth

LONDON SUBURBAN RAILWAYS

Caterham and Tattenham Corner
Clapham Jn. to Beckenham Jn.
Crystal Palace and Catford Loop
Holborn Viaduct to Lewisham
London Bridge to Addiscombe
Mitcham Junction Lines
South London Line
West Croydon to Epsom

STEAMING THROUGH

Steaming through Cornwall
Steaming through East Sussex
Steaming through the Isle of Wight
Steaming through Surrey
Steaming through West Hants
Steaming through West Sussex

COUNTRY BOOKS

Brickmaking in Sussex
East Grinstead Then and Now

SOUTH COAST RAILWAYS

Ashford to Dover
Bournemouth to Weymouth
Brighton to Eastbourne
Brighton to Worthing
Chichester to Portsmouth
Dover to Ramsgate
Hastings to Ashford
Ryde to Ventnor
Worthing to Chichester

SOUTHERN MAIN LINES

Bromley South to Rochester
Charing Cross to Orpington
Crawley to Littlehampton
Dartford to Sittingbourne
East Croydon to Three Bridges
Epsom to Horsham
Exeter to Barnstaple
Faversham to Dover
Haywards Heath to Seaford
London Bridge to East Croydon
Orpington to Tonbridge
Sittingbourne to Ramsgate
Swanley to Ashford
Three Bridges to Brighton
Tonbridge to Hastings
Victoria to Bromley South
Waterloo to Windsor
Woking to Southampton
Yeovil to Exeter

COUNTRY RAILWAY ROUTES

Andover to Southampton
Bath to Evercreech Junction
Bournemouth to Evercreech Jn
Burnham to Evercreech Junction
Croydon to East Grinstead
East Kent Light Railway
Fareham to Salisbury
Guildford to Redhill
Porthmadog to Blaenau
Reading to Basingstoke
Reading to Guildford
Redhill to Ashford
Salisbury to Westbury
Strood to Paddock Wood
Taunton to Barnstaple
Westbury to Bath
Woking to Alton

TRAMWAY CLASSICS

Bournemouth & Poole Tramways
Brighton's Tramways
Bristol's Tramways
Camberwell & W. Norwood Tramways
Croydon's Tramways
Dover's Tramways
East Ham & West Ham Tramways
Embankment & Waterloo Tramways
Exeter & Taunton Tramways
Greenwich & Dartford Tramways
Hampstead & Highgate Tramways
Hastings Tramways
Ilford & Barking Tramways
Kingston & Wimbledon Tramways
Lewisham & Catford Tramways
Maidstone & Chatham Tramways
North Kent Tramways
Southampton Tramways
Southend-on-sea Tramways
Thanet's Tramways
Victoria & Lambeth Tramways

OTHER RAILWAY BOOKS

Garraway Father & Son
Industrial Railways of the South East
London Chatham & Dover Railway
South Eastern Railway
War on the Line

MILITARY BOOKS

Battle Over Sussex 1940
Blitz Over Sussex 1941-42
Bombers over Sussex 1943-45
Military Defence of West Sussex

WATERWAY ALBUMS

Hampshire Waterways
Kent and East Sussex Waterways
London to Portsmouth Waterway
West Sussex Waterways

BUS BOOKS

Eastbourne Bus Story
Tillingbourne Bus Story

SOUTHERN RAILWAY ● VIDEOS ●

Memories of the Hayling Island Branch
Memories of the Lyme Regis Branch
War on the Line